OCS Study
MMS 2002-028

Observation of the Atmospheric Boundary Layer in the Western and Central Gulf of Mexico

Final Performance Report

I0438997

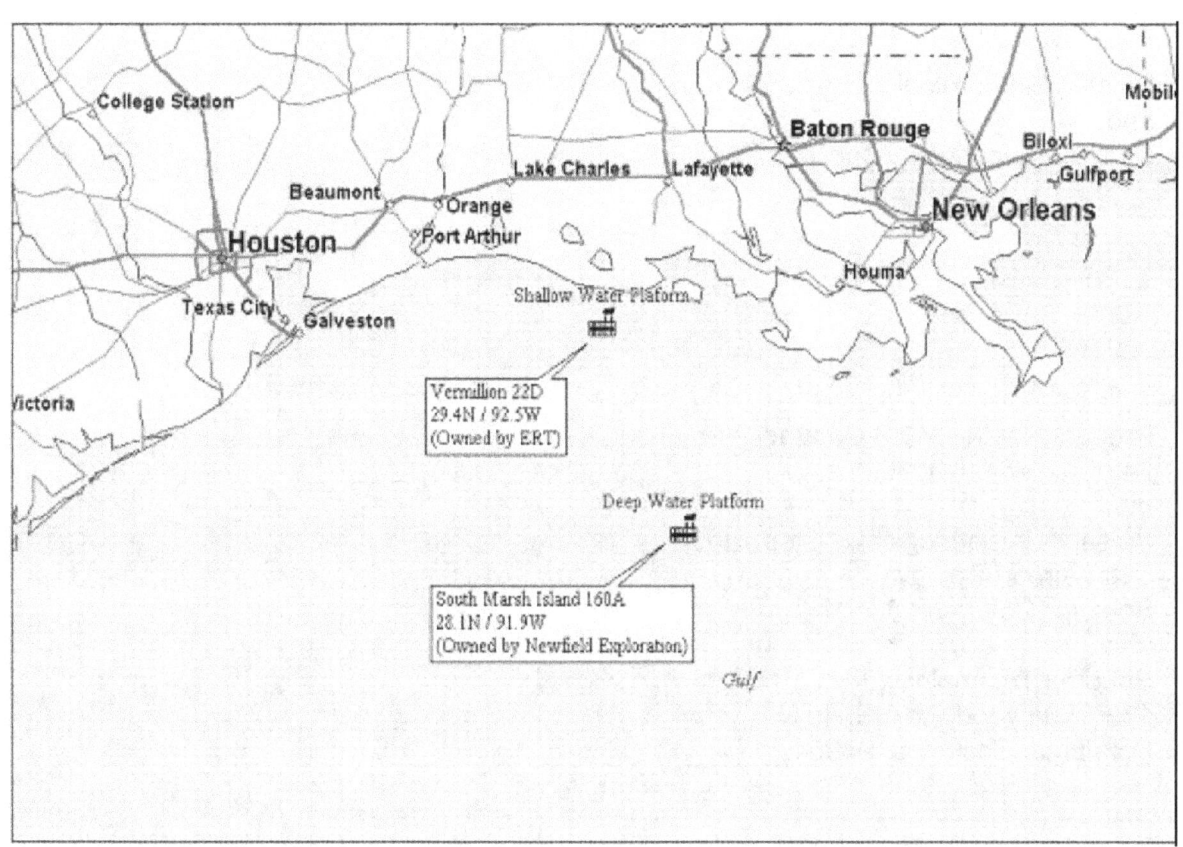

Shallow Water Platform

Vermilion 22D
29.4N / 92.5W
(Owned by ERT)

Deep Water Platform

South Marsh Island 160A
28.1N / 91.9W
(Owned by Newfield Exploration)

Gulf

MMS
U.S. Department of the Interior
Minerals Management Service
Gulf of Mexico OCS Region

OCS Study
MMS 2002-028

Observation of the Atmospheric Boundary Layer in the Western and Central Gulf of Mexico

Final Performance Report

Preparers

Vaisala Meteorological Systems, Inc.
and
Sonoma Technology, Inc.

Prepared under MMS Contract
1435-01-97-CT-30854
by
Vaisala Meteorological Systems Inc.
5600 Airport Boulevard
Boulder, Colorado 80301
and
Sonoma Technology, Inc.
1360 Redwood Way, Suite C
Petaluma, California 94954

Published by

U.S. Department of the Interior
Minerals Management Service
Gulf of Mexico OCS Region

New Orleans
August 2002

DISCLAIMER

This report was prepared under contract between the Minerals Management Service (MMS) and Vaisala Meteorological Systems Inc. This report has been technically reviewed by the MMS, and it has been approved for publication. Approval does not signify that the contents necessarily reflect the views and policies of the MMS, nor does mention of trade names or commercial products constitute endorsement or recommendation for use. It is, however, exempt from review and compliance with the MMS editorial standards.

REPORT AVAILABILITY

Extra copies of this report may be obtained from the Public Information Office (Mail Stop 5034) at the following address:

U.S. Department of the Interior
Minerals Management Service
Gulf of Mexico OCS Region
Public Information Office (MS 5034)
1201 Elmwood Park Boulevard
New Orleans, LA 70123-2394

Telephone: 504-736-2519 or 1-800-200-GULF

CITATION

Vaisala Meteorological Systems Inc. and Sonoma Technology, Inc. 2002. Observation of the Atmospheric Boundary Layer in the Western and Central Gulf of Mexico. U.S. Dept. of the Interior, Minerals Management Service, Gulf of Mexico OCS Region, New Orleans, LA. OCS Study MMS 2002-028. 122 pp.

ACKNOWLEDGMENT

This study was funded by the Minerals Management Services, U.S. Department of the Interior, Washington, D.C., under Contract Number 1435-01-97-CT-30854.

TABLE OF CONTENTS

LIST OF FIGURES

LIST OF TABLES

ACRONYMS AND ABBREVIATIONS

AGL	Above Ground Level
°C	Degrees Celsius
CD	Compact Disk
CDT	Central Daylight Time
CO	Contracting Officer
COTR	Contracting Officer's Technical Representative
CST	Central Standard Time
DCP	Data Collection Platform
ERL	Environmental Research Laboratory
GC	Gateway Computer
GFE	Government Furnished Equipment
GOES	Geostationary Operational Environmental Satellite
GPS	Global Positioning System
KHz	Kilohertz
km	kilometer
Max	Maximum
mb	millibar
Met	Meteorological
MHz	Megahertz
Min	Minimum
MMS	Minerals Management Service
m/s	meters per second
N	North
NA	Not Applicable
nsec	Nanoseconds
NCDC	National Climatic Data Center
NESDIS	National Environmental Satellite, Data, and Information Service
NOAA	National Oceanic and Atmospheric Administration
NTIA	National Telecommunications and Information Administration
NWS	National Weather Service
O&M	Operations and Maintenance
QA	Quality Assurance
QC	Quality Control
RASS	Radio Acoustic Sounding System
RC	Radar Computer
RF	Radio Frequency
RH	Relative Humidity
RWP	Radar Wind Profiler
sec	second
SMI	South Marsh Island 160A platform designator
STI	Sonoma Technology, Inc.
Tv	Virtual Temperature
VRM	Vermillion 22D platform designator
W	West

1.0   INTRODUCTION

This is the final contractor performance report on the data collection portion of the Boundary Layer Study in the Western and Central Gulf of Mexico, initiated by the Minerals Management Service (MMS), U.S. Department of the Interior.

Surface and upper-air meteorological data were collected at two off-shore platform sites for a continuous 40-month period from June 3, 1998 through October 2, 2001. Surface meteorological data measurements were made using identical suites of commercial in-situ sensors at each of the two platform sites. The surface data collected were wind speed, wind direction, air temperature, relative humidity, pressure, and sea surface temperature. Upper-air meteorological data measurements were made using an identical commercial remote-sensing boundary layer radar profiler at each of the two platform sites. The upper-air data collected were vertical profiles of wind direction, wind speed, and virtual temperature. Data measurements from each platform site were retrieved hourly throughout the 40-month data collection period via GOES satellite communications relay. All retrieved data were then quality controlled and reported monthly to MMS. At the end of the project, an electronic, assimilated data base of all surface and upper-air meteorological measurements recorded at both sites during the project was also prepared and delivered to MMS.

The prime contractor for this data collection project was the meteorological systems group that was under Radian International LLC as of the beginning of this MMS project and that subsequently became part of Vaisala Inc. during the project. This change resulted in no discontinuity in the contractor team performing the MMS project, other than the change of the name of the prime contractor. On September 22, 1997, MMS awarded the original contract for this project to Radian International LLC (an element of URS Corporation), and, effective October 29, 2001, MMS novated that contract to Vaisala Meteorological Systems Inc. (an element of Vaisala Inc.). For simplicity throughout this final performance report, prime contractor references are to "Vaisala" rather than spelling out in each reference that the prime contractor was originally "Radian" and changed to "Vaisala."

This report is organized to summarize project activities and results in essentially chronological order. In the order presented, the report documents the project methodology and its implementation, the site operations and data collection activities accomplished during each year of the project, the data measurement results achieved for the entire 40-month data collection period, and the end-of-project disposition status of the meteorological measurement equipment used. As reflected in the report, the project spanned a period of more than four years. This included approximately eight months of preparatory work to obtain and configure the measuring equipment and sites and to obtain necessary operating licenses, the 40-month data collection period itself, and finally a wrap-up period of several months to decommission sites, refurbish equipment, and compile the final data base and other project documentation.

2.0 METHODOLOGY AND IMPLEMENTATION

2.1 Goals and Objectives Specified by MMS at Project Start

2.1.1 Goals

For the Gulf of Mexico, present data sets poorly represent how temperature, winds, and mixing height vary vertically over the atmospheric boundary layer and free troposphere. Estimates come from two sources: 1) automated weather stations measuring meteorological variables in the surface layer; and 2) observational satellites sampling the boundary layer and free troposphere at a few select altitudes. Because these techniques generally do not accurately or precisely measure for a range of altitudes, empirical constants and relationships are used to approximate vertical variations in temperature, winds, and other boundary layer properties. However, direct observations more accurately describe vertical variations because the cited estimates contain many assumptions and simplifications.

Applications using these estimated winds, temperature, and mixing heights exist, but they contain uncertainties from above simplifications. For instance, the Minerals Management Service (MMS) applies such estimates in several ways when assessing changes in air quality from oil and gas production. The MMS requires meteorological inputs and computational routines in dispersion modeling. The MMS assessments use conceptual models of pollutant transport through the marine boundary layer and theoretical analysis on the marine boundary layer. The MMS then has an interest in collecting field observations of the vertical structure of the marine boundary layer because such observations would reduce uncertainties in environmental assessments.

Under this project, the MMS shall obtain field observations describing the vertical structure of the marine boundary layer over the Western and Central Gulf of Mexico for ongoing and future applications. The agency will accomplish this goal by establishing two (2) boundary layer profiler systems on offshore platforms for approximately three (3) years of data collection. The MMS requires acquisition, installation, and maintenance of equipment, data collection, data management, and routine reporting over the life of this project. The MMS will retain ownership during and after the time period.

Each system is to use existing, well-established technologies and procedures. Each system needs to make minimal demands on platform resources and produce no hazards to platform personnel or offshore radio transmissions.

This project will provide a valuable source of information to the National Weather Service (NWS) operations as the boundary layer observations are collected in real time and distributed. An arrangement will be set up to permit NWS direct access to the observations. The NWS will also supplement quality control and archive the observations at the National Climatic Data Center (NCDC).

2.1.2 Objectives

Accurately collect, record, and report meteorological observations for three years (later amended by MMS to 40 months) in the Western and Central Gulf of Mexico. These observations shall include temperature, atmospheric refractivity, and winds from the surface layer into the free troposphere. Surface data collected shall measure air and sea surface temperatures, pressure, winds, and humidity. Project task goals are as listed in Table 2-1.

Table 2-1. Project Task Goals

Task	Goal
1. Equipment	All equipment types listed in the contract are to be provided with careful consideration of cost-benefit trade-offs.
2. Field Plan	The most workable sites are to be identified and obtained. A comprehensive field plan is to be prepared and endorsed by MMS.
3. Deployment and Operations	Two sites are to be operated and maintained, in an accident-free manner, providing all required data types at 90% or greater capture level with diligent QA/QC and on-time reporting.
4. Discontinuation of Monitoring	Equipment is to be fully checked, appropriately refurbished, and relocated as directed by MMS in a timely manner after the data collection period.
5. All	The project is to be completed within the estimated costing and on a time schedule approved by MMS.

2.2 Project Planning and Organization

In coordination with MMS, the contractor developed and implemented two master planning documents that governed the management and operational detail of how the project was executed. These were the "Project Management Plan" and the "Field Plan" for Profilers and Data Collection for the MMS Boundary Layer Study in the Western and Central Gulf of Mexico. The project organization established in these planning documents, and as maintained throughout the project, is shown in Figure 2-1. The prime contractor, initially Radian International LLC and subsequently Vaisala Meteorological Systems Inc. , performed all functions shown within the CONTRACTOR organization, except the Principal Investigator and Data Processing and Reporting Team functions, which were performed by Sonoma Technology, Inc. (STI) under subcontract to the prime contractor.

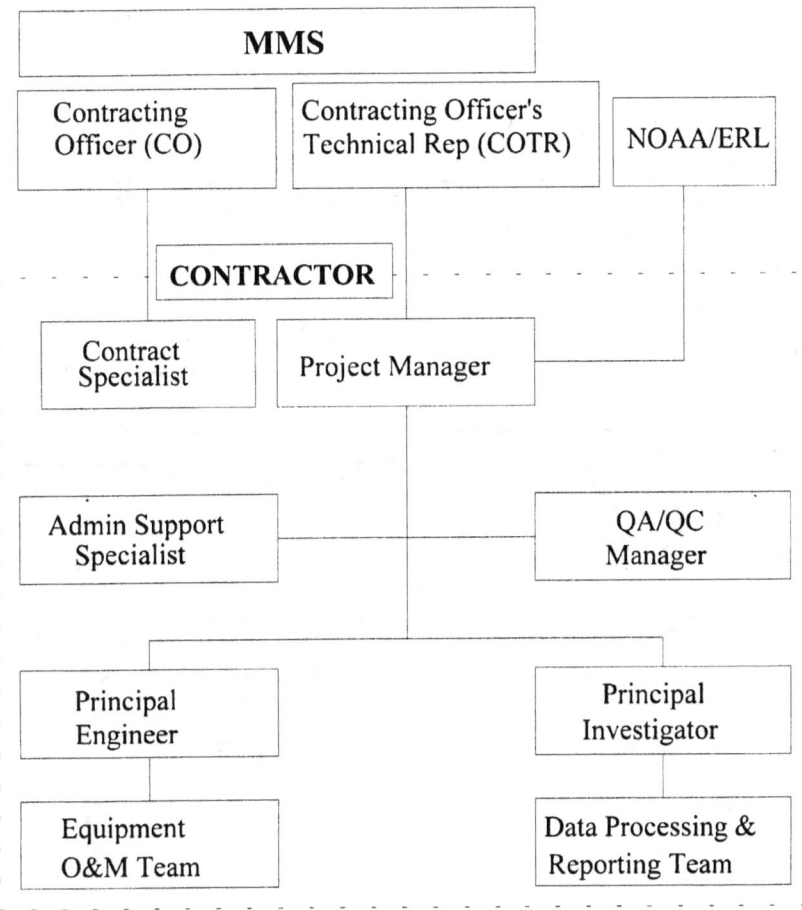

Figure 2-1. Project Organization Chart

2.3 Schedule

The project schedule, as originally planned and actually executed, is shown in Table 2-2.

Table 2-2. Project Schedule

Milestone	Originally Planned	Actually Executed[1]
Contract issued and work started to acquire and prepare sites and equipment (includes start of monthly management reports to MMS)	22 September 1997	22 September 1997
Start installation of equipment at sites.	February 1998	February 1998
Complete installation of equipment at sites.	February 1998	February 1998
Complete testing of equipment at sites (ready for start of data collection period).	March 1998	March 1998
GOES and RF frequency licenses received.	February 1998	May 1998
Start data collection period.	1 April 1998	3 June 1998
First monthly data report to MMS (monthly thereafter)	May 1998	July 1998
First draft annual report to MMS (annually thereafter)	30 September 1998	30 September 1998
Complete data collection period.	28 February 2001	2 October 2001
Removal of equipment from sites.	March 2001	November 2001
Final performance report, assimilated data set, and draft technical summary to MMS.	July 2001	February 2002

Note 1: Actually executed dates varied from originally planned dates because of an initial delay in receiving necessary site licenses and because MMS later extended the data collection period from 36 to 40 months.

2.4 Specifications

2.4.1 Meteorological Measurements Specifications

Table 2-3 lists project requirements established and implemented by meteorological data types, applicable measurement instruments used, measurement frequency, and measurement accuracy.

Table 2-3. Meteorological Measurements at Each Site

Measured Parameter	Sensor Manufacturer	Sensor Model	Range	Accuracy
Upper Air Measurements				
Wind Speed	Vaisala	LAP®-3000 RWP[1]	0 to 24 m/s (per beam)	±1.0 m/s
Wind Direction	Vaisala	LAP®-3000 RWP[1]	0 to 360 deg.	±10 deg.
Virtual Temperature	Vaisala	LAP®-3000 RASS[2]	5 to 40° C	±1.0° C
Surface Meteorological Measurements				
Wind Speed	RM Young	RMY 05305-5	0 to 40 m/s	±0.2 m/s
Wind Direction	RM Young	RMY 05305-5	0 to 360 deg.	±3.0 deg.
Air Temperature	Campbell Scientific, Inc.	HMP35C	-35 to +50.0° C	±0.5° C
Sea Surface Temperature	Everest Interscience, Inc.	4000.4GL	-40 to +100.0° C	±0.5° C
Relative Humidity	Campbell Scientific, Inc.	HMP35C	0 to 90% RH	±2% RH
			90 to 100% RH	±3% RH
Pressure	Vaisala	PTA-427	600 to 1060 mb	±0.6 mb

[1] Radar Wind Profiler(RWP)
[2] Radio Acoustic Sounding System (RASS)

2.4.2   Site Specifications

Each of two offshore oil platform sites in the Louisiana Gulf Coast was configured to fulfill the specifications in Table 2-3. The preferred locations of the respective two sites were established by MMS as approximately 10 km within the shoreline and approximately 50-80 km within the shoreline.

2.4.3   Logistics Responsibilities

The Program Manager was designated responsibility for monitoring all equipment and data handling logistics and for coordinating as appropriate with the MMS COTR.

The Principal Engineer was designated responsibility for all equipment logistics, including procurement, pre-deployment testing, shipping, installation, preventive and emergency maintenance, audits and calibrations, removal, refurbishment, and shipment to MMS storage.

The Principal Investigator was designated responsibility for all data handling logistics, including sensor operating parameters, data retrieval, data reasonableness checks, audit and calibration report reviews, data validation, reporting, and archiving. He performed these functions through the facilities and personnel of STI's dedicated Weather Operations Center in Petaluma, California and worked closely with the project QA/QC Manager.

The QA/QC Manager monitored data and report quality and kept the Program Manager appraised of status, including any problems and recommended corrective action.

2.5   Selection of Sites

The site selection process was completed as the first step in field project preparation. A location in shallow water was needed to measure how the marine boundary layer is affected by the land/sea breeze mechanism. Such a location was estimated to be within 10 km from the shoreline. A location in deep water was needed to measure how the marine boundary layer is affected by interaction between advecting air masses and colder waters in the Gulf of Mexico. Such a location was believed to be near the 200 m isobath and approximately 75 km from the shoreline. Locations of the chosen sites are depicted in Figure 2-2.

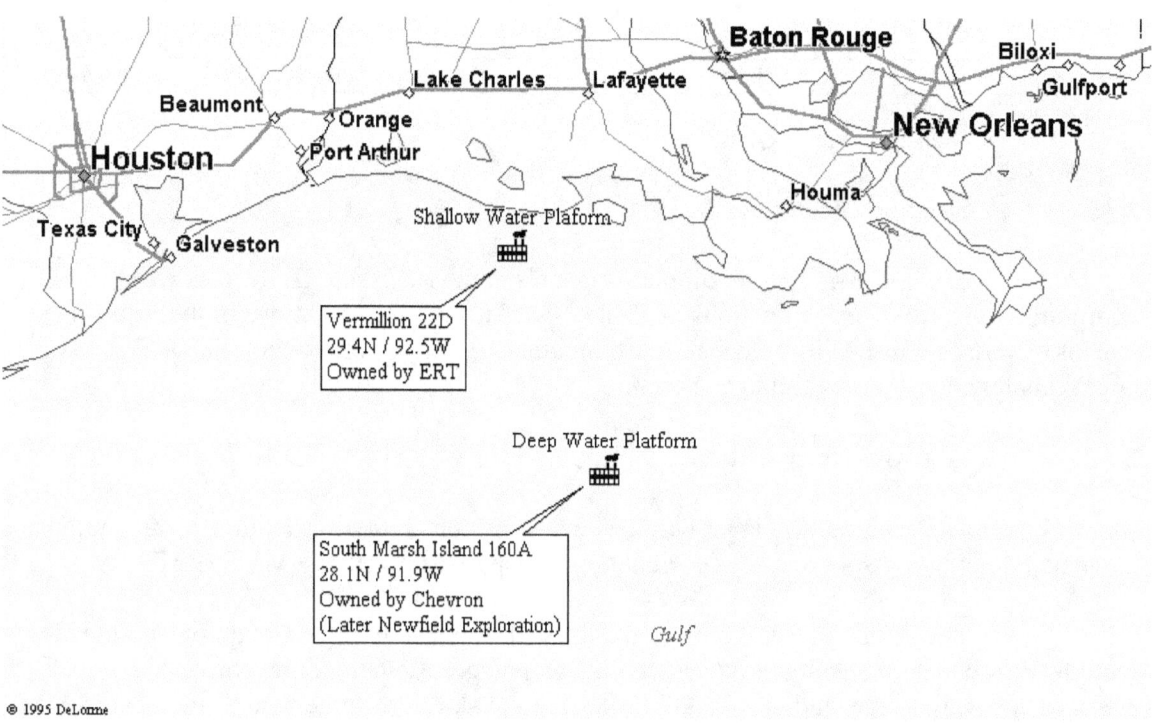

**Figure 2-2. Locations of Chosen Offshore
Meteorological Measurements Sites**

In addition to preferred geographical location, oil platform site selection criteria included:

- Manned platforms are far preferable to unmanned.

- Adequate open-deck space (10 m x 10 m) is required for the radar antenna, located within 150 ft. of a shelter.

- The shelter must have reliable mains power and environmental control for electronics.

- The platform should have a microwave telephone communications link.

- There should be no obstructions or towers above 5 deg. from the surface of the wind profiler.

The Principal Engineer performed two site surveys, via helicopter, of the platforms in lease blocks recommended by the MMS COTR. The first survey, on 9/30/97, evaluated nine platforms in the southern part of the South Marsh Island (SMI) block and four platforms in the Ship Shoal block. From these, SMI160A was selected as the optimal deep-water site and the platform owner, Chevron, subsequently provided approval for MMS use of this manned platform. Later in the project, Chevron sold the SMI160A platform to Newfield Exploration, who also allowed the MMS equipment to remain on the platform and continue operations.

Eleven unmanned platforms were evaluated in the shallow-water East and West Cameron lease blocks. After review with the MMS COTR, a second survey was conducted on 10/22/97, during which an additional seven shallow-water platforms in the Vermillion lease block and six shallow-water platforms in the northern part of the South Marsh Island lease block were evaluated. In coordination with the MMS COTR, it was decided that the preferred shallow-water platform site was Vermillion 22D because it meets the siting criteria from an equipment perspective and it is best located to capture sea breeze information. Approval from the platform owner, ERT, was subsequently obtained for use of this manned platform.

2.6   Site Equipment and Communications

Figure 2-3 illustrates the site equipment subsystems that were installed on each platform site, and the interconnectivity of these subsystems. The subsystems are:

- RWP (LAP®-3000 and RASS);
- Surface meteorological sensors;
- Computers; and
- Communications Interfaces.

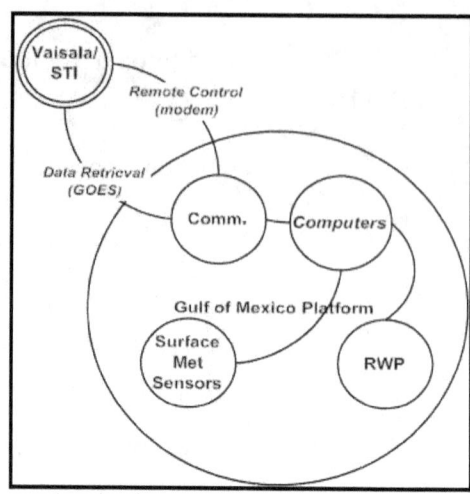

Figure 2-3. Site Equipment Subsystems and Interconnectivity

2.6.1   Radar Wind Profiler (RWP)

Figure 2-4 illustrates the interconnectivity view of the RWP (LAP®-3000/RASS). The LAP®-3000 RWP is a remote sensing Doppler radar that produces a profile of the vertical and horizontal winds in clear air up to approximately three kilometers above ground level (atmospheric dependent). The profile includes wind speed and direction. The LAP®-3000's Radio Acoustic Sounding System (RASS) provides a profile of virtual temperature up to approximately 1.2 kilometers above ground level (atmospheric dependent). The radar profiler produces wind and reflectivity data by transmitting signal pulses in the vertical and up to four pointing directions that are each tilted in elevation about 15 degrees off vertical and are each separated by 90 degrees in azimuth. The operating frequency is 915 MHZ (32.8 cm wavelength). After transmitting a pulse signal, the profiler receives the return signals that are reflected by the turbulence in the atmosphere. From these returns, the radar profiler computes the wind speed and direction for a selected number of heights above the ground.

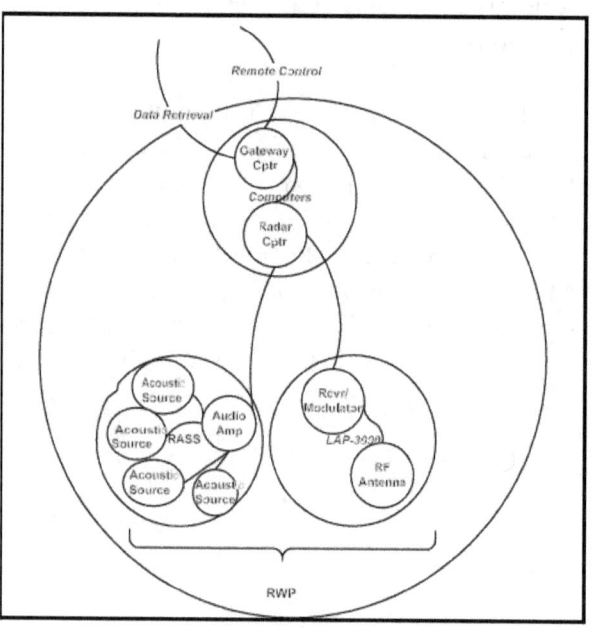

Figure 2-4. RWP Subsystem Interconnectivity

2-8

The radar profiler produces virtual temperature data by automatically halting wind finding for a preprogrammed period of RASS operation. During RASS operation, the four acoustic sources are activated and the vertical beam of the radar is used to track the RASS acoustic transmission in order to measure the speed of sound for a selected number of heights above the ground. Speed of sound data are then automatically converted to virtual temperature data by the LAP®-3000. Table 2-4 shows the initial sampling configurations for the radar wind profilers and RASS for this project. These configurations were adjusted throughout the project to optimize performance based upon atmospheric and environmental conditions at each profiler site.

Table 2-4. Sampling Configurations for RWP

Specification	Winds	T_v	Surface Met
Averaging period (min)	55	5	60
Reporting interval (min)	60	60	60
Time standard	CST	CST	CST
Time convention	Begin	Begin	Begin
Vertical resolution (m)	~100 (low mode) ~200 (high mode)	60	-
Minimum altitude (m agl) VRM[1]	131	120	-
Maximum altitude (m agl) VRM[1]	4934	1260	-
Minimum altitude (m agl) SMI[1]	131	135	-
Maximum altitude (m agl) SMI[1]	4920	1275	-

[1]Altitude referenced as "agl" (above ground level) means above platform level.

The LAP®-3000 provides continuous real-time atmospheric wind and virtual temperature data. The LAP®-3000 operates unattended. For more on the general theory and physics of how this type of instrument measures virtual temperature and resolves winds, see Ecklund et al., 1990.

The LAP®-3000 is a system of interrelated components. The RF antenna (including final amplifier unit) and RASS antennas are positioned outside an environmentally controlled shelter area and all other components are positioned inside the environmentally controlled shelter. The system is configured with an Uninterruptible Power Supply to help protect the profiler from changes in AC power supply voltage, including AC power loss of up to 20 minutes duration.

The LAP®-3000 operates using two computers, a Radar Computer and a Gateway Computer, both positioned within the environmentally-controlled shelter. The Radar Computer controls overall radar operation and data analysis, and transfers measured vertical profiles of wind and virtual temperature data to the Gateway Computer. The Gateway Computer is connected to a Global Positioning System (GPS) device that provides accurate time updates, which the Gateway Computer also relays to the Radar Computer. The Gateway Computer also receives surface meteorological data measurements from the data logger, which is connected to the surface meteorological sensors. The Gateway Computer provides external communication through a modem and a GOES interface. Figure 2-5 shows the interconnectivity and data storage access of the Radar Computer and Gateway Computer. Profiler supervision and control by remote connection through the telephone modem is accomplished using remote access software ProComm.

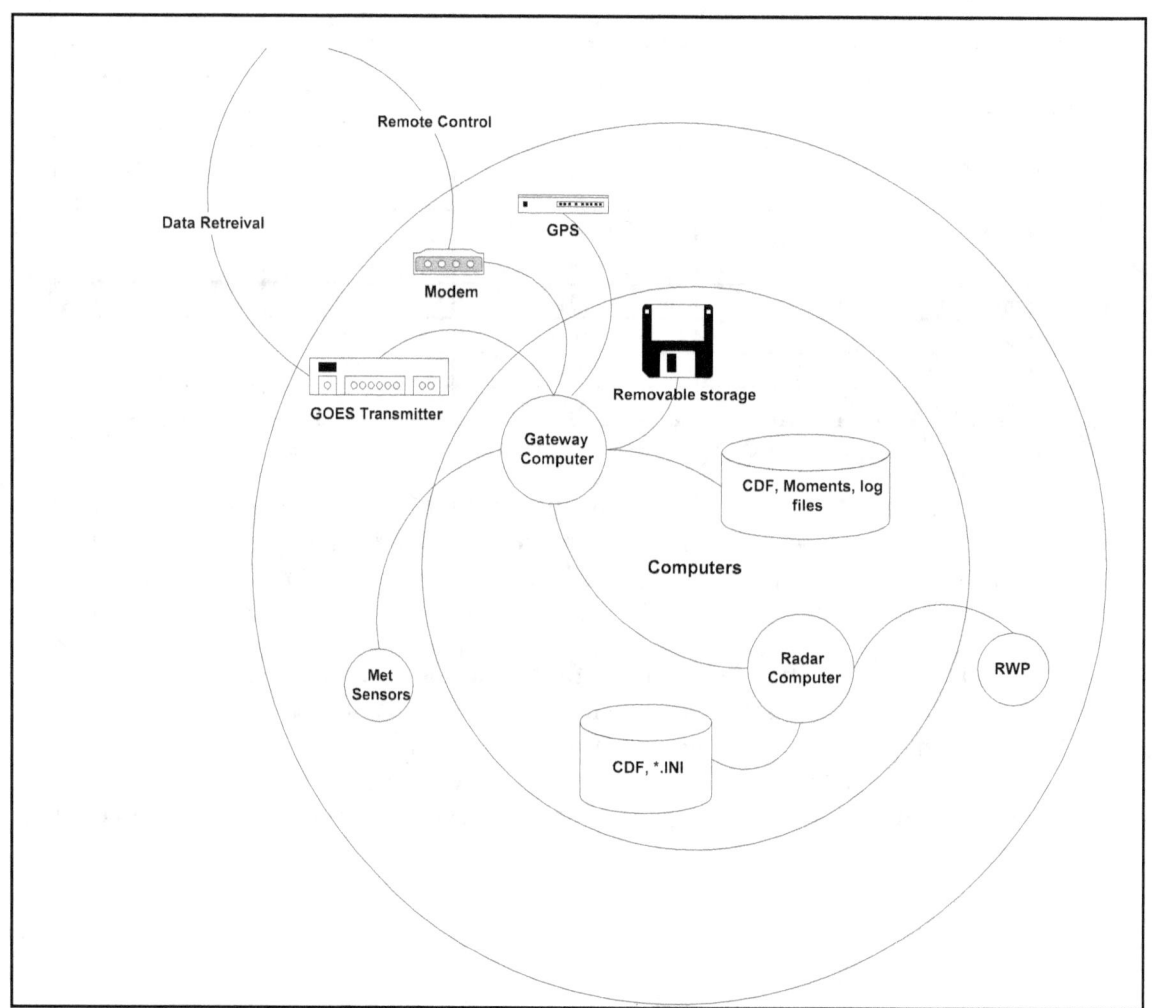

Figure 2-5. RWP Computers Interconnectivity and Data Storage

2.6.2 Surface Meteorological Sensors

The surface meteorological measurements at the two platform sites included: wind speed and direction; air and sea-surface temperature; relative humidity; and pressure.

Figure 2-6 illustrates the interconnectivity of the surface meteorological sensors installed at each site.

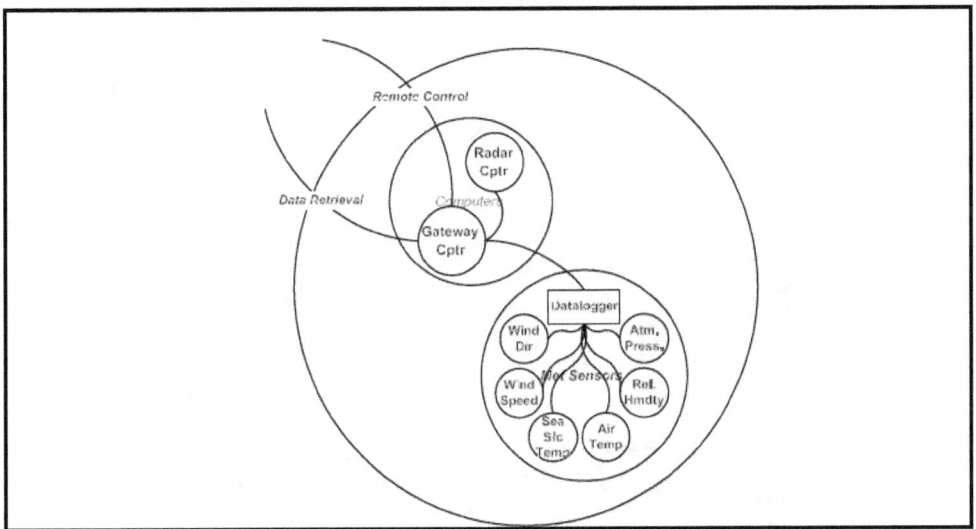

Figure 2-6. Surface Meteorological Sensors Interconnectivity

The specific surface meteorological equipment to be installed on each platform site is listed in Table 2-5.

Table 2-5. Surface Meteorological Sensor Model Numbers

Item Description	Model
Wind Direction/Speed	RMY 05305-5
Air Temperature/R.H.	CSI HMP35C
Sea Surface Temperature	4000 4GL
Pressure	PTA 427
Data Logger	CR10
Calibration	A.I.R. Barometer
Calibration	Rotronic T/RH Probe

2.6.3   Site Communications and Data Flow

2.6.3.1   Site Communications

Site communications as shown in Figure 2-7 included:

- A data uplink to Geostationary Orbiting Environmental Satellite (GOES) that served as the primary link for transferring hourly data.

- A telephone/modem served as a secondary data link and for diagnostics and system configuration.

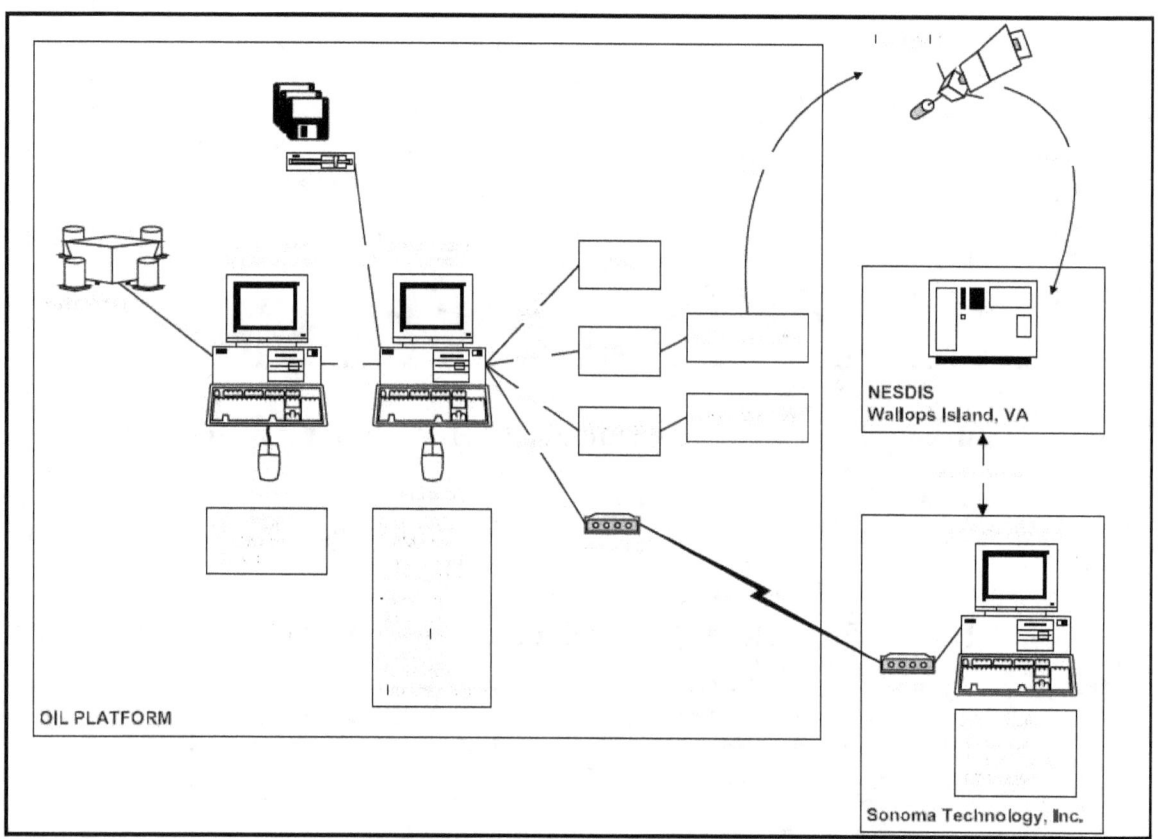

Figure 2-7. Site Communications

2.6.3.2   Data Flow

At each platform measurement site, the profiler and surface meteorological data were collected every hour on the Gateway Computer. Then, selected data were compressed into a data packet and were sent by the site's GOES Data Collection Platform (DCP) over the assigned GOES transmission channel to the NESDIS site at Wallops Island, Virginia. The assigned GOES transmission channel, authorized by NESDIS for this MMS project, permitted transmission of up to two minutes duration from each site at specified times after each hour. A copy of the transmitted data was stored on the NESDIS file server in Virginia for FTP Internet download or dial-in modem access for at least 72 hours. The project's data processing and reporting team at STI automatically downloaded the data as soon as it became available and performed reasonableness checks to identify problems. The GOES data were also retransmitted via domestic satellite (DOMSAT) to a downlink at the NOAA laboratories in Boulder, Colorado. Data flow detail is illustrated in Figure 2-8.

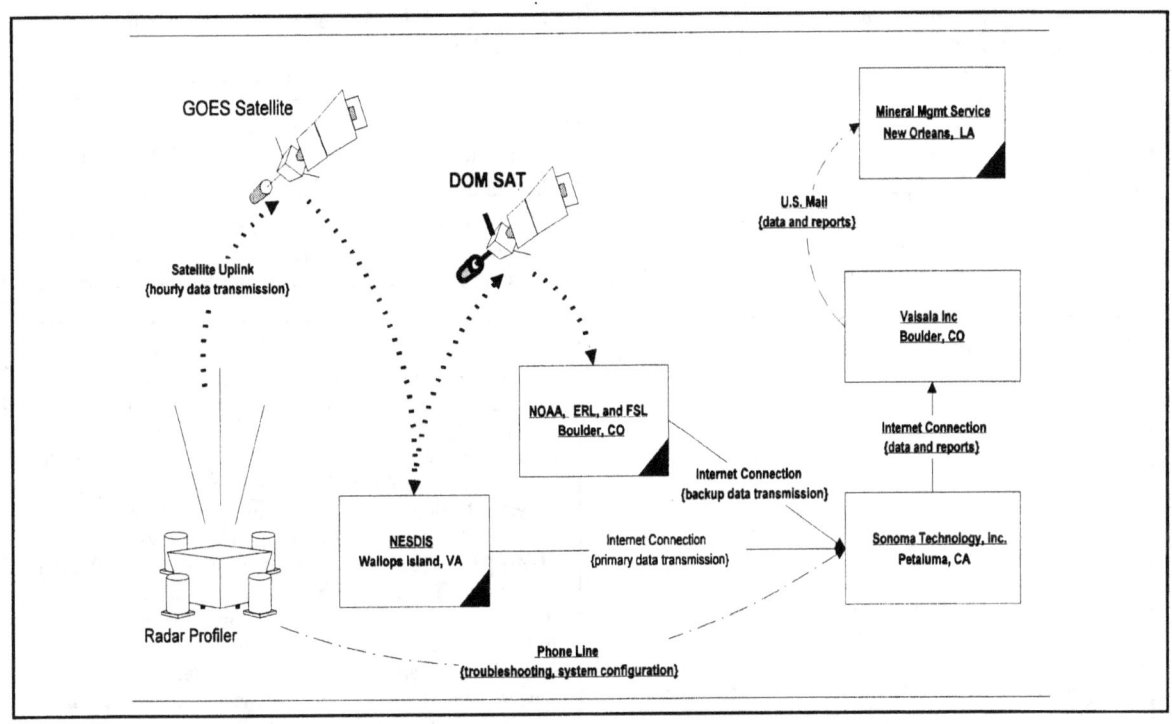

Figure 2-8. Data Flow

2.7 Site Obstacles and Hazards

The establishment of meteorological equipment and radar profilers on platforms in the Gulf of Mexico created some unique obstacles and hazards that needed special safeguards as summarized in Table 2-6 below.

Table 2-6. Obstacles and Hazards with Safeguards Employed

Obstacle or Hazard	Safeguards
Down time due to platform environmental problems such as air conditioner failure or inadvertent disruption by platform personnel.	Use of manned platforms and fostering of good relationships with platform workers. Use of standard computers that incorporate a lockable front panel behind which are the power switches, floppy drives, and a keyboard lock.
Restrictions on data retrieval/QA due to loss of long-line communications.	Redundant communications and enhanced on-site data storage capacity.
Severe weather (lightning, heavy rains, and high speed winds) and marine environment effects on exposed equipment.	Humidity protection for electronics (in environmentally controlled shelter/office); enhanced anchoring (welding and strong guy wiring); lightning spikes or rods; electricity surge protection; and in-line surge protection for all lines leading from the shelter to the antenna. For the surface met. equipment, an opto-isolating interface in the shelter to provide isolation for the computer.
RASS noise is potential concern.	RASS audio is only a hazard inside the RASS antenna enclosures. Warning signs are posted. Fiberglass enclosures make the RASS sources inaccessible to personnel.
RF radiation potential concern.	Within ANSI standards even immediately above the antenna. Clutter fences and warning signs provide additional safety. Fiberglass enclosures make the antenna inaccessible to personnel. Under the antenna assembly, a metal cover seals off this vulnerable side of the antenna from both the weather and people. The July 1982 RF exposure limits set by the American National Standards Institute (ANSI) in ANSI C95.1-1982 are a maximum safe exposure level, at 915 MHZ, of 3 mW/cm2. The LAP-3000 antenna system has a signal strength of 2 mW/cm2 directly over the antenna array, a location that is inaccessible to personnel because of the clutter screen assembly. The exposure level is further reduced by the vertical pointing of the antenna and the clutter screen assembly, which attenuate the signal strength an additional 30 to 50 dB (max 2 mW/cm2).

Table 2-6. Obstacles and Hazards with Safeguards Employed (Cont'd)

Obstacle or Hazard	Safeguards
Interference with platform operations/personnel.	The LAP®-3000 and RASS do not interfere with platform activities, including cellular phone communications or aircraft navigation. All support desired from platform-owner companies and their personnel will be coordinated and approved in advance. This will include: some transportation support (on company-scheduled boat or helicopter); some on-platform support (overnight accommodations, crane support and welding support during installation and removal); occasional trouble-shooting calls to platform personnel to perform simple system checks; etc.
Personnel tripping on cables.	Cables across walkways minimized and a conduit or cover used to protect the cables. High visibility tape or paint to warn workers of cables' presence. Power supplies in the system drop to 0 VDC if the cables are shorted or damaged, preventing any threat to personnel.
Walking into or tripping over guy wiring.	Guy wires marked with high visibility spiral wrap.
Deteriorating environmental protection steps.	Periodic maintenance visits by project team technicians and cooperation of platform workers to call the project team if an obvious deterioration is noted (e.g., a loose or broken guy wire, A/C failure, etc.).
Loss of data due to system failures.	Use of radar UPS, auto-restart, remote control operation, electric power surge protection, battery backup for data logger, and selected sparing of equipment and parts. The radar electronics plug into a Toshiba UPS which tolerates a wide AC input range (+10%,-30%). This unit also supplies a fully rectified output with line filtering which gives 100% isolation from AC line noise and surges. The UPS will provide 20 minutes of backup in the event of a total loss of power. When the battery capability is exceeded, the system will shut down without damage to electronics. When power is restored, the system will boot normally and resume sampling without operator input. Emergency maintenance visits will be performed as needed to restore operations and routine maintenance visits will be performed on a scheduled basis to help prevent possible failures.
Corrosion and part failure due to corrosion from moisture and salt spray.	Whenever possible, parts have been upgraded to marine grade stainless steel to resist corrosion. Additionally, bottom covers are installed on the antenna unit to minimize the penetration of corrosive sprays to the antenna feed system and components. The marine version of the surface ind sensor has been installed to provide be available perfor-mance for this sensor given the harsh environment. Bi-annual inspections include assessment of the hardware so that small problem due to corrosion can be corrected in the early stages.

Note: Although not an "obstacle or hazard" another limiting factor in operating a radar profiler on an offshore platform is that seawave motion (which produces a Doppler shift) can interfere with wind profile neasurements in the lower altitudes above the profiler's antenna. This occurs when radar sidelobe energy is reflected vack to the profiler's antenna from the moving seawaves, producing return signals that are much stronger than those produced by the winds. The degree and persistence of sea clutter (interference) varies with seawave height and directional orientation. It also depends on whether the platform structure extends avove the height of the radar antenna, causing radar energy to be reflected off the structure to the seawaves.

2.8   Equipment and Site Operating Procedures

2.8.1   Equipment Preparation Testing

Testing of the equipment was done by the Principal Engineer in two stages: 1) pre-deployment mockup systems testing at the factory prior to shipment and 2) on each platform following installation. The installation technician followed prescribed steps to ensure the systems were running properly. This process included inspection of the signal outputs, calibrating the meteorological sensors, and a brief data audit. A degree of testing was done through remote communications whereby the data management team conducted data reasonableness checks daily. Data reasonableness checks were performed through remote communications with the sites while the installation team was still on each platform, and over an approximate one-week period after installation. The Principal Investigator confirmed the successful completion of this data review testing prior to the official start of the three-year data collection period.

2.8.2   Installation

The Principal Engineer led the team that installed the equipment at both platform sites. Installation of each LAP®-3000 required one day for the major assembly and a second day to complete final details. The installation process included the following actions:

- Equipment was sent via commercial van lines to nearest on-shore holding facility.

- In preparation of a boat trip, arrangements were made for platform personnel availability to haul the equipment from the boat to the platform's deck, for a welder to be present, and a technician to be at the platform to receive the equipment. Use of the platform crane and a certified operator were required to lift the crates from boat to deck.

- The project installation team installed the profiler antennas, RASS assemblies, and met sensors on each platform at predesignated and agreed to locations.

- The electronics were housed inside a prior agreed-to office or other air conditioned enclosure with proper electric power access.

- Once the installation was complete, guy anchors were welded to the platform deck. Platform personnel were needed to assist for the short time it took to attach the guy plates. Cables from the profiler antennas, RASS, and meteorological equipment support posts were routed to the office where the electronics were housed using appropriate anchoring and protective coverings for personnel safety.

2.8.3   **Operations and Maintenance**

The Operations and Maintenance (O&M) program, managed by the Principal Engineer included :

- A shakedown operations test prior to formal data collection period;

- Scheduled site equipment checks;

- Unscheduled (emergency) site equipment repairs; and

- End-of-program equipment checks.

2.8.3.1   **Site Audits**

During all scheduled or emergency platform site visits after installation, site audits were conducted using a Platform Site Audit Checklist, which included:

- Overall evaluation of the condition of the station;

- Operating condition of each sensor;

- Placement and/or alignment of each sensor;

- Reasonableness of sensor outputs with atmospheric conditions;

- Data collection, processing, and archiving functionality; and

- Data acquisition system clocks are compared against a standard.

2.8.3.2   **Scheduled Site Visits**

Scheduled site visit equipment checks were performed at approximately six-month intervals at both platforms. The visiting O&M team member used the Platform Site Audit Checklist for scheduled visits and the LAP®-3000 O&M Manual to guide the maintenance tasks.

The visiting Equipment and O&M team member took required test equipment and spare parts on each platform visit. Problems found were corrected during the visit if possible, or were corrected as soon as possible during a follow-up emergency site visit if they could not be corrected during the scheduled site visit.

Copies of the completed checklist for each visit were distributed to the QA/QC Manager for review and were placed in project files immediately after the visit.

2.8.3.3 Remote Problem Resolution and Emergency Site Visits

The Data Processing and Reporting team attempted to resolve any problem(s) detected by performing remote system resets or, as appropriate, by obtaining telephone assistance from on-site platform personnel. If remote problem solving did not work, the Data Processing Reporting Team passed the problem resolution task to the Principal Engineer for resolution.

The Principal Engineer then attempted to resolve the problem remotely. As required, the Principal Engineer then arranged for an Equipment O&M team member to perform an emergency site visit by helicopter.

All problems noted and their resolution were documented for review by the QA/QC Manager and in the project file. The Platform Site Audit Checklist for emergency visits was completed and distributed immediately after the visit. For problems resolved remotely, Data Processing and Reporting Team personnel or the Principal Engineer, as appropriate, prepared and distributed a problem resolution report.

If an emergency site visit was performed within about 30 days prior to a scheduled site visit, it fulfilled the requirement of the next scheduled site visit if the Equipment O&M team member performing the emergency visit was able to also complete a scheduled visit Platform Site Audit Checklist, if all problems were resolved during the emergency visit, and if no new problems were noted.

2.8.4 QA/QC Program

The QA/QC program implemented for this MMS project included the equipment and data checks summarized below.

2.8.4.1 Instrument Calibrations and Checks

During scheduled site visits calibrations and checks of the surface meteorological, LAP®-3000, and RASS upper-air equipment were performed and documented to ensure that the instruments were operating according to manufacturer's guidelines. A formal calibration involved measuring the "conformance to or discrepancy from a specification ... for an instrument ... and an adjustment of the instrument ... to conform to the specification" (U.S. EPA, 1989). A calibration of the surface meteorological equipment was straightforward and followed U.S. EPA guidelines. A calibration of the radar profiler and surface meteorological equipment was more complex since it is difficult to directly compare winds to a known standard. Instead, a series of diagnostic checks were performed to verify that the electronics and individual components of a system are working properly. This approach conforms to the EPA's guidelines for the quality assurance and management of PAMS upper-air meteorological data (Lindsey et al., 1995).

2.8.4.2   Review of Calibrations and Checks

Once the on-site calibrations and checks were completed, results of these checks were sent to the QA/QC Manager for review. For example, if the calibration showed that the surface wind direction sensor was mis-aligned by 10°, all wind direction data were adjusted by 10°. All calibrations were applied to the data before they were officially released.

2.8.4.3   Reasonableness Checks of the Data

Daily throughout the study, data reasonableness checks were made to ensure the measurements produced make sense. This was performed using nearby meteorological information from surface towers or other upper-air sensors, as available. A project team meteorologist at STI was responsible for reviewing these upper-air data and comparing them to nearby measurements.

This check was not meant to evaluate whether or not the data meet the manufacturer's data specifications, but rather as a "reasonableness check" to identify problems such as:

- Component failures;
- Incorrect operating/sampling parameters;
- Instrument failures;
- Antenna azimuth angles mis-measured.

2.8.4.4   Data Validation

Data validation is the process of determining the quality of the data and identifying observations with errors, biases, or physically unrealistic values (Lindsey et al., 1995). Without data validation, questionable or erroneous data might be used for modeling or analysis purposes and in decision making. A meteorologist or another trained person who has a basic understanding of the meteorological phenomena and the operating principles of the instrument performed data validation weekly. The data validation process involved identifying physically, spatially, or temporally inconsistent observations ("outliers") and assigning QC codes to each data point to indicate its validity. There are several stages or "levels" in the data validation process:

Level 0 data validation consisted of raw data obtained directly from the data instruments in the field. Level 0 data are unedited and unreviewed. These data have not received any adjustments for known biases or problems that may have been identified during preventive maintenance checks or audits. These data were used to monitor the instrument operations on a daily basis.

Level 0.5 data validation consisted of using software to perform quantitative screening of the data. For the radar profiler and RASS data, quantitative checks were performed by the software-screening program developed by Wuertz and Weber (1989) that examines the temporal and vertical continuity of the data to identify possible outliers. For the surface meteorological data, STI's SurfDat software was used to automatically screen the surface data using quantitative criteria developed by the EPA (U.S. EPA 1989).

Level 1 data validation took place after the data had been collected and passed the Level 0.5 data validation. During this validation step, the data received qualitative reviews for accuracy, completeness, and internal consistency. Qualitative checks were performed by meteorologists and trained personnel who manually reviewed the data for outliers and problems. Quality control flags, consisting of numbers or letters, were assigned to each datum to indicate its quality. A list of QC codes is given in Table 2-7. The surface and upper-air data were only considered at Level 1 after calibration reports had been reviewed and any adjustments, changes, or modifications to the data had been made.

Table 2-7. Quality Control (QC) Codes for Surface and Upper-Air Data

QC Code	QC Code Name	Definition
0	Valid	Observations that were judged accurate within the performance limits of the instrument.
1	Estimated	Observations that required additional processing because the original values were suspect, invalid, or missing. Estimated data may be computed from patterns or trends in the data (e.g., via interpolation).
2	Calibration applied	Observations that were corrected using a known, measured quantity (e.g., instrument offsets measured during audits).
3	Unassigned	Reserved for future use.
4	Unassigned	Reserved for future use.
5	Unassigned	Reserved for future use.
6	Failed automatic QC check	Observations that were flagged with this QC code did not pass screening criteria set in automatic QC software.
7	Suspect	Observations that, in the judgment of the reviewer, were in error because their values violated reasonable physical criteria or did not exhibit reasonable consistency, but a specific cause of the problem was not identified (e.g., excessive wind shear in an adiabatic boundary layer).
8	Invalid	Observations that were judged inaccurate or in error, and the cause of the inaccuracy or error was known (e.g., winds contaminated by ground clutter or a temperature lapse rate that exceeded the autoconvective lapse rate). Besides the QC flag signifying invalid data, the data values themselves should be assigned invalid indicators.
9	Missing	Observations that were not collected.

2.9 Data Storage and Handling

2.9.1 On-Site Data

The instrument systems on each platform created and stored three types of data files: moments data, consensus data, and surface meteorological data. This section describes the contents of these data files.

2.9.1.1 Moments Files

The moments data files contain individual 20-30 second wind profiles with information about the Doppler shift, the spectral width, the noise power, and the signal-to-noise ratio measurements. These data may be needed in the future to diagnose the instrument performance, re-compute winds with a shorter averaging period (e.g., 15 minutes), and to compute the refractive index structure function (C_n^2). The moments data consist of two types of files: header and data. The header files contain project and site-specific information and the data files contain the actual data. These data files are in a binary format and are produced by the radar software. The combined size of the header and data moments files are approximately 1000 to 1500 KB per day. These data are stored on the Radar Computer in the "C:\RADAR\DATA" directory with a ".MOM" file extension. The moments file naming convention is:

> DYYJJJA.MOM (moments data)
> HYYJJJA.MOM (moments header)

Where: YY = Year
           JJJ = Julian day
           A = File sequencer in 1 MB steps

For example, D98011A.MOM is a moments data file for January 11, 1998.

2.9.1.2 Consensus Data Files

There are two types of consensus files: wind and virtual temperature. The radar software produces both types of consensus files every hour by processing and averaging the 20-30 second moments data. The LAP®-3000 uses a technique referred to as "consensus averaging" to compute hourly wind profiles (Fischler and Bolles, 1981). Using this technique, a radial velocity is determined for each beam direction and each measurement height every 20-30 seconds, and the software selects the largest subset of the radial velocities measured during the hour that fall within a user-selectable velocity window (typically 2 m/s). The hourly horizontal wind direction and speed is then computed for each measurement height using the chosen subset of radial velocities. If at least 60 percent of the radial velocities do not fall within 2 m/s of each other, no winds would be reported at that altitude for that hour.

The consensus data are in an ASCII text format and contain hourly averaged wind and virtual temperature profiles. The size of each type of consensus data file is approximately

100 to 200 KB per day. The consensus data files are stored on the gateway computer in the "C:\GATEWAY\DATA" directory with a ".CNS" file extension. The consensus data file naming conventions are:

WYYJJJ.CNS (wind data)
TYYJJJ.CNS (virtual temperature data)

Where: YY = Year
JJJ = Julian day

For example, W99308.CNS is a wind file for November 4, 1999.

2.9.1.3 Surface Meteorological Data Files

The surface meteorological data include wind speed and direction, air temperature, sea-surface temperature, relative humidity, and pressure. These surface data are stored in the Campbell Scientific Inc. (CSI) surface meteorological data logger. Software located on the gateway computer communicates with the CSI data logger and retrieves the latest surface meteorological data every hour. The raw surface meteorological data are stored in an ASCII text file in a comma separated variable (CSV) format. This file is located on the gateway computer in the "C:\CSI" directory with a ".DAT" extension. The surface meteorological data file naming convention is:

SIDH.DAT

Where: SID = Three letter site identification code
H = Hourly averaged data

2.9.2 Remote Collection

Three pathways were used to receive data remotely. The primary data pathway was through the GOES satellite transmission, the secondary link was via modem, and the third method of data collection was via the routine maintenance trips.

2.9.2.1 GOES Satellite

As noted in Section 2.6.3.2, data were automatically transmitted every hour through a GOES satellite link. Within the constraints of the GOES time allotments, the data sent via GOES consisted of the parameters listed in Table 2-8.

Table 2-8. Radar Profiler and Surface Meteorological Data Sent via GOES

Parameter	Units	Reporting Convention
Site Information		
Site ID	N/A	AAA
Date and begin time of consensus period	yy mm dd hh mm ss (in CST)	xx xx xx xx xx xx
Surface Meteorological Data		
Averaging Interval	60 minutes	XX
Software Version	N/A	X.XX
Year	N/A	XXXX
Julian Day (day of year)	N/A	XXX
Hour	CST	XXXX
Wind Speed	Meters per second (m/s)	XX.X
Wind Direction	Degrees true	XXX.X
Resultant Wind Speed	Meters per second (m/s)	XX.X
Resultant Wind Direction	Degrees true	XXX.X
Std. of Wind Direction	Degrees	XXX.X
Ambient Temperature	Degrees Celsius (°C)	XX.X
Sea Surface Temperature	Degrees Celsius (°C)	XX.X
Relative Humidity	Percent	XXX.X
Atmospheric Pressure	millibars (mb)	XXXX.X
Upper-Air Winds (Mode 1)		
Pulse width	100 meters	XXXX
Number of Range Gates	25	XX
Gate Spacing	100 meters	XXXX
Height	Meters (m)	XXXX
Wind Speed	Meters per second (m/s)	XX.X
Wind Direction	Degrees from true north	XXX.X
Vertical Velocity	Meters per second (m/s)	XX.X
Signal-to-Noise Ratio (vertical beam)	Decibels (dB)	XXX
Upper-Air Winds (Mode 2)		
Pulse width	400 meters	XXXX
Number of Range Gates	25	XX
Gate Spacing	200 meters	XXXX
Height	Meters (m)	XXXX
Wind Speed	Meters per second (m/s)	XX.X
Wind Direction	Degrees true	XXX.X
Vertical Velocity	Meters per second (m/s)	XX.X
Signal -to-Noise Ratio (Vertical Beam)	Decibels (dB)	XXX

Table 2-8. Radar Profiler and Surface Meteorological Data Sent via GOES (Cont'd)

Parameter	Units	Reporting Convention
Upper-Air Virtual Temperature		
Pulse Width	60 meters	xxxx
Number of Range gates	20	xx
Gate Spacing	60 meters	xxxx
Height	Meters (m)	xxxx
Virtual Temperature	Degrees Celsius (°C)	xx.x
Virtual Temperature (Corrected)	Degrees Celsius (°C)	xx.x
Vertical Velocity	Meters per second (m/s)	xx.x

Note: x=numbers, and A=characters.

2.9.2.2   Modem Transmission

The dial-up modem pathway served as a redundant backup to access and download data in the event that the primary GOES transmission was unsuccessful. Another important aspect of the modem connection was to remotely control the instruments to troubleshoot, configure, maintain, and conduct diagnostics.

2.9.2.3   Field Data

A project O&M team member collected the field data from each site during the scheduled site maintenance visits. The field data consisted of ZIP disks with the moments, consensus, and surface meteorological data. This was mailed to STI, where its receipt was recorded and the data and information were archived.

2.9.3   Archives

Archiving of the surface and upper-air data was critically important to ensure that the data were not lost, destroyed, or corrupted. A reliable archive was updated frequently and included redundant backups. Two copies of all data for the project was maintained at all times and data were archived at the earliest possible opportunity. The two major data sets that were archived included the hourly GOES data and the field data received from the scheduled regular maintenance visits.

As the hourly GOES data were received at STI, they were logged and stored in an MS ACCESS database. This database resided on STI's HUB computer. It was automatically backed-up each night across a local area network (LAN) onto a separate hard drive. The database was archived to a compact disk (CD) and a ZIP disk every month. The CD remained at STI and the ZIP disk will be sent to Vaisala to provide a redundant offsite backup of the data on different media.

When the project O&M team member sent the field data to STI after a scheduled site visit, approximately every six months, the data from the ZIP disks were logged and backed-up onto a computer hard-drive and to a CD. The CD remained at STI as part of the archive, and the ZIP disks were sent to Vaisala to provide offsite storage of the data on different media.

2.9.4 Use in Reports

The project team used the GOES data and other log/status data to compile a monthly project data report that was sent to MMS. Each monthly report included a summary of operations, an explanation of the data formats, and the data. Figure 2-9 shows the contents outline of the monthly data report.

---

1. INTRODUCTION

    Table 1. Site locations and information

2. SUMMARY OF OPERATIONS

2.1 Sampling Configurations.

    Table 2. Sampling configurations of sensors used.
    Table 3. Specifications of sensors used.

2.2 Data Completeness

    Table 4.   Data Capture Rates for Both Sites During the Reporting Period
    Table 5.   Data Recovery for Valid Level 1.0 RASS Data at VRM
    Table 6.   Data Recovery for Valid Level 1.0 Low-Mode Wind Data at VRM
    Table 7.   Data Recovery for Valid Level 1.0 High-Mode Wind Data at VRM
    Table 8.   Data Recovery for Valid Level 1.0 RASS Data at SMI
    Table 9.   Data Recovery for Valid Level 1.0 Low-Mode Wind Data at SMI
    Table 10. Data Recover for Valid Level 1.0 High-Mode Wind Data at SMI
    Table 11. Events at Affected the Data Recovery and/or the Data Quality

2.3 Data Adjustments

    Table 12. Data adjustments

3. DATA FORMATS

    Table 13. Description of the data fields in the "WINDdata" table
    Table 14. Description of the data fields in the "RASSdata" table
    Table 15. Description of the data fields in the "SURFdata" table

Attachment: CD containing the month's observations.

Figure 2-9. Outline of Monthly Project Data Report to MMS

3.0   DATA COLLECTION OPERATIONS

Project team activities spanned the timeframe from September 1997 through February 2002 and included the three project phases of preparing for data collection operations, conducting data collection operations, and performing follow-up tasks after the completion of data collection operations. As originally specified by MMS, the planned data collection period was to be 36 months. As implemented, the data collection period began on June 3, 1998, and was therefore scheduled for completion on June 2, 2001. However, prior to that scheduled completion date, MMS elected to change the data collection period to 40 months in order to expand the data base to fully encompass the time period of the complementary Breton Aerometric Monitoring Program (BAMP) data collection project. The BAMP project was sponsored by the Off-Shore Operator's Committee. It included six data measurement sites, five of which were also on off-shore platforms in the Gulf of Mexico near Breton Island. The BAMP data collection period was from September 2000 through September 2001. As a result of the extension of the data collection period from 36 to 40 months, MMS data collection operations that began on June 3, 1998 were completed on October 2, 2001.

Data collection operations conducted are summarized in Sections 3.1 through 3.4 below in approximately annual increments. Section 3.1 covers the period leading up to the June 3, 1998 start of the 40-month data collection period and it also includes the first four months of actual data collection operations. Sections 3.2 and 3.3 document the second and third full years of the project, all of which were part of the 40-month data collection period. Finally, Section 3.4 covers the final year of the data collection period, and also includes the approximately 4-month follow-up period during which the sites were de-commissioned, equipment was refurbished, the full project data base was compiled, and project reports were prepared.

3.1   Project Year One Activities (09/22/97 - 9/30/98)

Work accomplished and results achieved during the first year of the project, September 22, 1997 through September 30, 1998, are detailed below.

Meteorological monitoring systems were installed on two platforms in the northern Gulf of Mexico as illustrated in Figure 3-1. SMI160A was owned by Chevron at the beginning of this MMS project, but was sold to Newfield Exploration during the project. The sensors on each platform included a 915 MHZ boundary layer profiler to measure vertical profiles of wind speed and direction, a 2 KHz RASS unit to measure virtual temperature profiles, and a suite of surface meteorological instruments. A GOES DCP (Data Collection Platform) was also installed at each site to transmit hourly data via satellite communications to the project data management facility.

Activities during the first year included:

- Preparing and testing the radar profilers;

- Purchasing additional surface meteorological sensors;

- Obtaining GFE sensors and other hardware;

- Integrating the sensor and communications components;

- Developing procedures for data collection, analysis, and reporting;

- Modifying hardware and software to meet special MMS field conditions and communications requirements;

- Selecting and preparing oil platform sites;

- Obtaining RF licenses for communications and profiling operations;

- Installing the systems on the oil platforms;

- Operating and maintaining the data collection systems; and

- Submitting monthly status and data reports.

Installation and testing of the meteorological monitoring systems at the two platform sites was completed during March 1998, but the monitoring systems were shut down temporarily while awaiting necessary RF licenses. The originally planned three-year data collection period started on June 3, 1998. An overview of the first year of the project is shown in Figure 3-2, and a description of the activities of this startup period is provided in the sections below.

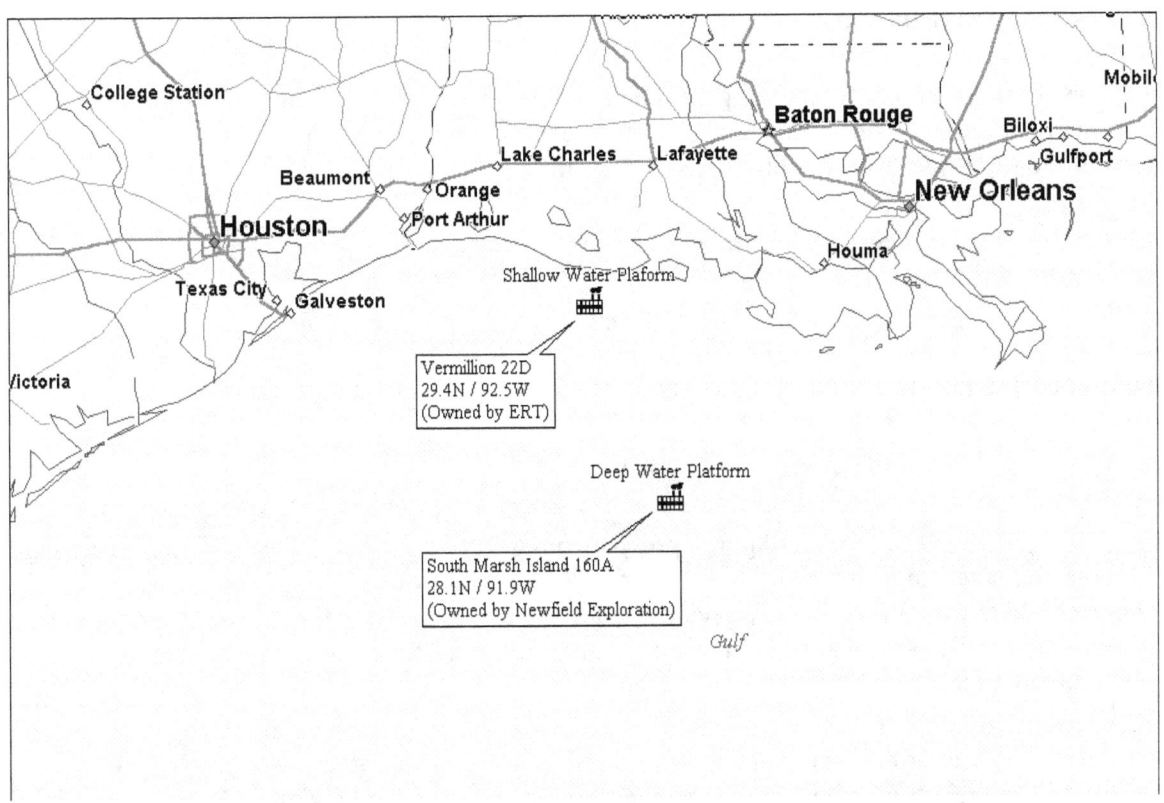

Figure 3-1. Location of Selected Monitoring Sites

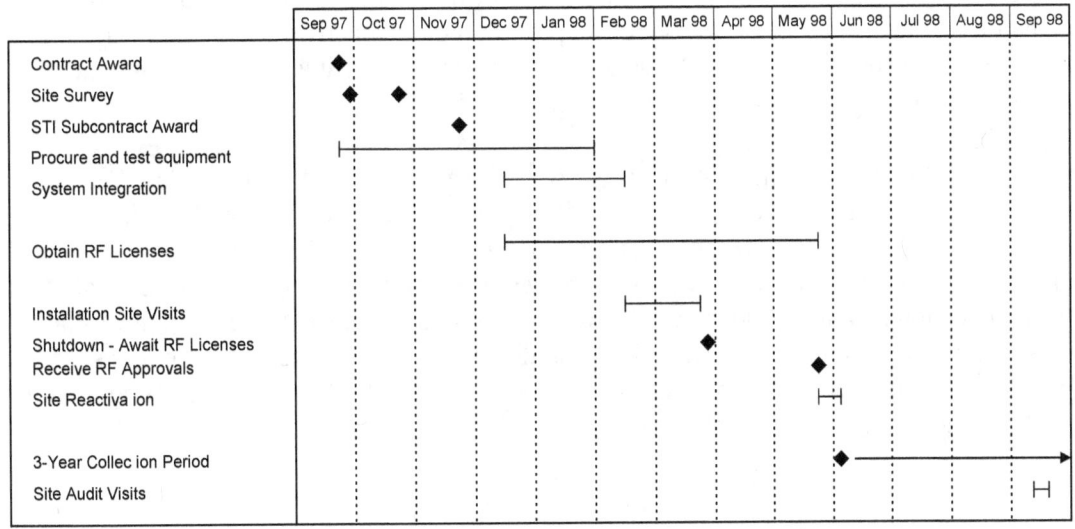

**Figure 3-2. Principal Activities of MMS Boundary Layer Study
September 1997 to September 1998**

3.1.1　　　　Management

MMS and contractor participants implemented a highly effective project team working relationship, using e-mail and telephone conferences to coordinate implementation actions and to resolve potential problems as they arose.

3.1.1.1　　　　Personnel

Table 3-1 shows the key personnel participants in the project during the first year. As noted in that table, Dr. Alexis Lugo-Fernandez replaced Bill Hutzel as MMS COTR during the first year of the project.

3.1.1.2　　　　Communications and Coordination

Authority for all required project team decision actions to ensure timely, efficient, and competent accomplishment of all work under the contract was vested in the Program Manager. Authority for day-to-day decision making was delegated to the Principal Engineer for all equipment-related matters and to the Principal Investigator for all data collection and processing matters.

The flow of internal team communications and coordination began with the issuance of written Project Instructions by the Program Manager and a kick-off meeting of all projects participants hosted by the Program Manager. Project contractual requirements, the responsibilities of all product team members in fulfilling those requirements, as well as detailed scheduling and budget planning were discussed in detail. Team meetings were held at the call of the Program Manager on an as-required basis. The Principal Engineer and Principal Investigator convened meetings with project personnel supporting their respective functional areas on a regular basis to ensure the continued flow of effective and timely internal communications throughout the project.

Meetings of the project key personnel were convened on a scheduled basis at the end of each month at the call of the Program Manager or as requested by the Principal Engineer or Principal Investigator. These meetings provided assurances for timely flow of communications within the leadership of the project team and for the coordination on all matters requiring decision actions. Regularly scheduled monthly meetings included a review of all actions completed during the prior month which then served as the basis for monthly status reports issued by the Program Manager to MMS. Projected activities for the ensuing month were also reviewed at each monthly meeting.

Table 3-1. Project Year One Key Personnel

Project Function	Person Performing Function	Comments
MMS Contracting Officer (CO)	Wally Adcox	
MMS Contracting Officer's Technical Representative (COTR)	Alex Lugo-Fernandez	Replaced Bill Hutzel, who served as COTR at the beginning of the project.
Program Manger	Gary Zeigler	Radian (later Vaisala)
Principal Investigator	Tim Dye	STI
Principal Engineer	Carlton Schneider	Radian (later Vaisala)

All formal external communications and coordination by project team members were directed through the Program Manager. Informal communications and coordinating with personnel and agencies outside the project team were encouraged by individual team members as necessary to ensure effective accomplishment of the routine work within the responsibility of the respective team participant. Issues that arose during such informal external contacts were immediately reported through the project management chain to the Program Manager for formal resolution.

3.1.1.3   Record Keeping

The project contract file, including copies of all correspondence with the MMS Contracting Officer was maintained in the office of the Contract Specialist.

A copy of all documentation related to project accomplishment was maintained in the office of the Program Manager. These documents included all project directives, reports of trips and meetings, record copies of all written deliverables submitted to MMS, and copies of all written correspondence between the Program Manager and the MMS COTR.

Data collection and processing, chain of custody, and other quality assurance records were maintained by the Principal Investigator. These records served as the basis of monthly and annual reporting, as well as other formal submissions.

Equipment testing, installation, operation, maintenance, and quality assurance records were maintained by the Principal Engineer. The Principal Engineer also maintained a log of all scheduled and unscheduled site visit activities and the results thereof. These records served as the basis of monthly and annual reporting, as well as other formal submissions, that were initiated by the Principal Engineer, through the Program Manager, to MMS as contract deliverables.

Photographic records of all significant project activities were taken by project team members, under the direction of project key personnel, as inputs to MMS under the "Presentation Slide Sets" deliverable requirement of the contract.

3.1.2 Site and Equipment Preparation Logistics

3.1.2.1 Site Selection

On September 22, 1997 the MMS COTR provided the project team a list of candidate oil platforms to serve as data collection sites for the boundary layer study. He requested that the shallow water site be selected on a line between Cameron and Sabine Pass, and that the deep water site be selected on the 150m to 200m isobath between the Ship Shoal and Garden Banks blocks. Additional criteria included:

- Manned platform, if possible, to help assure continuous operations;

- Adequate space for the radar profiler antenna;

- Minimal obstructions or towers which would cause radar profiler interference clutter;

- Environmentally controlled shelter space available for electronics; and

- Shelter within 150m of the radar profiler antenna location.

On September 30, 1997 a project team field engineer surveyed the candidate platforms to assess their suitability as data collection sites. He first flew through the area to make a quick visual inspection of the platforms, looking for adequate space for the radar profiler antenna, presence of a shelter for the electronics, and the absence of structures which could cause radar clutter. He took pictures of the platforms and visited the most promising deep water platform. A suitable shallow water platform was not located on this visit.

The area was visited again on October 22, 1997 to further attempt to locate a usable manned platform near the coast. Several workable candidates were identified.

After coordination with the MMS staff and the platform operators, the following two platforms were selected for the study:

1) South Marsh Island 160A, operated by Chevron, as the deep water site; and

2) Vermillion 22D, operated by ERT, as the shallow water site.

3.1.2.2   RF Licenses

RF licenses were required for the GOES satellite data up-link and for the wind profiler operating frequency.

- The profiler data was transmitted using a two-minute per hour channel of the NOAA/NESDIS Geostationary Operational Environmental Satellite (GOES) system. Allocation of the channel from NESDIS and permitting from NTIA to transmit to the GOES satellite at 402 MHZ were required.

- The wind profiler measurements were based on radar pulses centered at 915 MHZ. Permission from NTIA to operate the two profilers in the Gulf of Mexico in this band was required.

Contractor project team members coordinated with NOAA ERL staff on procedures for communicating profiler data via GOES, and also on the steps required to request GOES allocations. The necessary applications for the GOES channel allocations were completed and submitted to NESDIS in December 1997. On January 20, 1998 an allocation for one minute per hour was received. The project team immediately went back to NESDIS and received the necessary two minute per hour allocation, as originally requested.

The RF license applications for operating at 402 MHZ and 915 MHZ were completed and submitted through MMS to the Department of the Interior in January 1998.

In February, the project team arranged to temporarily borrow GOES channels from the NOAA Aeronomy Laboratory so that system integration and testing could proceed while waiting for the NTIA approvals.

In the last week of March 1998, the Department of the Interior submitted the RF applications to NTIA. Soon thereafter, NOAA withdrew the temporary loan of the GOES channels because they were required for a NOAA field project.

The RF broadcast approvals were received from NTIA on May 26, 1998, and the planned three-year data collection period began a few days later, on June 3, 1998.

3.1.2.3   Equipment

The radar wind profilers employed in this MMS project were manufactured at Radian's (now Vaisala's) assembly plant in Boulder, CO. Each was integrated with surface meteorological sensors and data communications components from MMS and from commercial vendors. Custom modifications to the two systems were made to adapt to the harsh environmental conditions expected on the platforms and also to support the unique data communications requirements. The components were also tested at the Boulder facility before deployment to ensure the reliability of the fielded systems. Table 3-2 lists the equipment deployed.

Table 3-2. Meteorological Equipment Specifications

Measured Parameter	Sensor Manufacturer	Sensor Model	Sensor Specifications	
Wind Speed	RM Young	RMY 05305-5	Accuracy:	±0.2 m/s
			Range:	0 to 40 m/s
Wind Direction	RM Young	RMY 05305-5	Accuracy:	±3°
			Range:	0 to 360°
Temperature	Campbell Scientific, Inc.	HMP35C	Accuracy:	±0.5°C
			Range:	-35° to +50.0°C
Relative Humidity	Campbell Scientific, Inc.	HMP35C	Accuracy:	±2% RH
			Range:	0-90% RH
			Accuracy:	±3% RH
			Range:	90 to 100% RH
Pressure	Vaisala	PTA-427	Accuracy:	±0.6 mb
			Range:	600 to 1060 mb
Sea Surface Temperature	Everest Interscience, Inc.	4000.4GL[1]	Accuracy:	±0.5°C
			Range:	-40°C to 100°C
Upper-air Wind Speed	Vaisala	LAP®-3000 RWP[2]	Accuracy:	±1.0 m/s
			Range:	0 to 24 m/s (per beam)
Upper-air Wind Direction	Vaisala	LAP®-3000 RWP[2]	Accuracy:	±10°
			Range:	0 to 360°
Upper-air Virtual Temperature	Vaisala	LAP®-3000 RASS[3]	Accuracy:	±1.0°C
			Range:	5°C to 40°C

[1] An infrared remote sensor mounted on a platform guardrail and pointed downward at the water surface
[2] Radar Wind Profiler (RWP)
[3] Radio Acoustic Sounding System (RASS)

The key steps in assembling and integrating the equipment suites for the two platforms were:

- Prepare and test the two 915-MHZ wind profilers;

- Add custom modifications to the profilers for platform operation;

- Adapt Gateway software to support surface met sensors and GOES data transfer;

- Purchase Radian-procured portion of surface met equipment;

- Receive and integrate MMS-provided surface met components;

- Procure GOES Data Collection Platforms;

- Write custom software modules to compress data for GOES data links; and

- Integrate and test complete systems at the contractor's Boulder facility.

3.1.2.4   Data Processing

The data processing and communications tasks planned for the project included preparing the data at the sites, transmitting the data back through GOES, receiving the data at the STI Weather Operations Center, analyzing and storing the data, and submitting data reports. To prepare for these tasks, the following steps were accomplished between the start of the project and March 1998:

- Adapt Gateway computer to ingest surface meteorological data;

- Write Gateway module to generate compressed data packets for GOES transmission;

- Configure Gateway to send hourly data packets to NESDIS via the GOES RF up-link;

- Develop procedures to retrieve data packets from NESDIS computer;

- Develop procedures to decode and analyze the data;

- Specify, in coordination with the MMS COTR, the content and format of monthly data reports; and

- Develop software and procedures to support data archival and report generation.

3.1.2.5   Installation Activities

As described in Section 3.1.2.1, the two platform sites were selected on the basis of information gathered during two visits to the Gulf of Mexico area in September and October of 1997, in coordination with MMS and platform operations staff.

Special requirements for the two sites were identified. For example, there was limited space in the air conditioned shelter at SMI160A for the Radar and Gateway Computers. Also shared telephone connections to the computers at each site were arranged. The positioning of electronic and antenna components and the resulting cabling requirements were determined for each site.

The equipment was shipped to the Louisiana coast in early February 1998. The monitoring equipment was installed at the SMI160A site on February 16-19, and at VRM 22D on February 20-22. The spares were positioned in Lafayette, LA on February 23, 1998.

Project team members made two return visits to the sites on 3-8 March 1998 and 24-26 March. During these visits a number of identified instrumentation issues were addressed and resolved. Although all equipment installation had been completed, the two sites had to be placed in a temporary shutdown mode on March 25, 1998 when NOAA had to withdraw their GOES channel loan (as noted in Section 3.1.2.2 of this report).

The RF broadcast licenses requested from NTIA by the Department of the Interior for this MMS project were received on May 26, 1998. Site reactivation was started on May 27 and the sites were visited on June 1-3. Equipment readiness checks were completed and both sites were operational as of the afternoon of June 2 and the data collection period began on June 3, 1998.

3.1.3   Site Operations and Maintenance

The planned three-year data collection period began on June 3, 1998. Regularly scheduled site visits were planned at six-month intervals, with the first such visit scheduled in September 1998.

No unscheduled site visits were required between June and September, 1998. Data collection continued without interruption for all sensors on both platforms during this period, except for a period of about four days in late September due to Hurricane Georges (as described below).

Tropical storm Earl passed through the Gulf of Mexico in early September. Both platforms were evacuated for several days. Before departure, the VRM22D platform's power was shut off causing 38 hours of radar data loss spanning 1-2 September. The surface meteorological data at VRM22D was, however, successfully captured as its battery powered backup was sufficient to last through the passage. No data were lost at the SMI160A platform as power there was not shut down upon evacuation.

As shown in Table 3-3, the first scheduled visit to the sites following the start of the data collection period was performed 14-17 September 1998. This visit included equipment audits and several corrective maintenance actions.

Hurricane George passed through the area in late September. Both sites were evacuated and the power was turned off at both sites. Power outages caused loss of 98 hours of radar data at VRM22D spanning 26-30 September and 94 hours of radar data at SMI160A spanning 25-29 September. The surface data collection continued uninterrupted because the battery-backup was able to keep this portion of the system working during the four-day evacuation period at each platform.

At SMI160A, GOES transmission of the data did not resume when the platform operators returned to the platform and restored power to the system on September 29. One of the operators accidentally broke the power switch on the GOES Data Collection Platform unit while restoring power. It was confirmed that the profiler was collecting data. An unscheduled maintenance visit was planned for October 9, 1998 to install the spare GOES unit on the SMI160A platform so that the failed unit's power switch can be repaired. As documented in section 3.2.3 of this report, that visit was successfully completed.

Table 3-3 lists all site visits performed during the first year of the project, both before and after the June 3, 1998 start of the data collection period.

Table 3-3. Project Year One Site Visits

Visit Date	Site(s) Visited	Visit Type	Visit Tasks Completed
9/30/97	Multiple	Scheduled	Surveyed candidate sites
10/22/97	Multiple	Scheduled	Surveyed candidate sites
2/16/98 – 2/19/98	SMI160A	Scheduled	Installed equipment
2/20/98 – 2/22/98	VRM22D	Scheduled	Installed equipment
3/03/98 – 3/08/98	VRM22D & SMI160A	Scheduled	Tested/audited equipment and communications
3/24/98 – 3/26/98	VRM22D & SMI160A	Scheduled	Tested /audited equipment and communications Note: After completion of all equipment installation and testing, as listed above, both sites were ready for operation, but the start of the data collection period was then delayed until 6/3/98 pending receipt of necessary site RF operating licenses (permitting radar profiler and GOES up-link RF transmissions).
9/14/98 – 9/17/98	VRM22D & SMI160A	Scheduled	Performed periodic equipment audits
			At VRM22D, restored GOES transmissions by clearing a Gateway Computer interrupt
			At both VRM22D and SMI1601, adjusted the RASS configuration setting to increase the expected range of upper air temperatures to be potentially measured.

3.1.4 Data Measurements

3.1.4.1 Description

The radar profiler was pre-programmed to take measurements continuously, and to alternate between recording vertical profiles of wind and recording vertical profiles of virtual temperature. During periods in which it is recording wind measurements, it was also pre-programmed to do so using alternating short (700 nsec) and long (2800 nsec) transmission pulses. The resultant "dual-mode winds" produced included "low-mode winds" and "high-mode winds." Low-mode winds are the wind measurements made using the short transmission pulse. Advantages of low-mode winds are that they start at the lowest possible altitude above the radar profiler and that they have the best possible vertical resolution. High-mode winds are the wind measurements made using the long transmission pulse. The advantage of the high-mode winds is that they extend to the highest possible altitude above the radar profiler.

The Gateway computer on each platform collected data from the radar profiler, the surface meteorological instrument datalogger, and the GPS receiver. Once each hour, the latest data are packed into a compressed format and transmitted through the GOES satellite link to a database on the NOAA/NESDIS system in Wallops Island, VA.

Automated procedures in the STI weather operations facility were used to retrieve and unpack the data files. The STI staff reviewed the data daily to ensure that all of the collection systems were operating correctly. At the end of each month, the prior month's data were processed to quality-stamp any suspect and invalid measurements. A monthly data report was then generated. The validated monthly data were also loaded into a database archive.

3.1.4.2   Data Capture Rate

The data capture rate measures the up-time of the integrated data collection and communications systems at each site. It is defined using:

Data Capture Rate = (NumRec/NumPos)*100

where:

NumRec = number of hours of data received at STI during the reporting period
NumPos = number of hours of data possible during the reporting period
(for example, 30 x 24 = 720 in a 30 day reporting period)

As of the September 30, 1998 end of the first year of the project, data rates for June, July and August 1998 were available (and data for September 1998 were being processed).

The data capture rates for June-August 1998 for the VRM22D site are shown in Table 3-4. The data capture rates for the same period for the SMI160A site are shown in Table 3-5. The goal of the MMS program was to achieve a capture rate of 90% or higher. The actual average capture rate for all sensors for the initial three-month collection period was 97.5%.

Table 3-4. Data Capture Rates for VRM22D Site, June-August 1998

Month	Upper Air Winds	Upper Air T$_v$	Surface Met
June 1998	99.3%	99.3%	99.3%
July 1998	93.8%	93.8%	93.8%
August 1998	97.0%	97.0%	97.0%

Table 3-5. Data Capture Rates for SMI160A Site, June-August 1998

Month	Upper Air Winds	Upper Air T$_v$	Surface Met
June 1998	98.2%	98.2%	98.2%
July 1998	97.4%	96.2%	97.5%
August 1998	99.7%	99.7%	99.6%

3.1.4.3   Data Recovery Rate

The data recovery rate is defined as the percentage of valid data captured by each instrument while the integrated system is operational. It is calculated using:

Data Recovery Rate = (NumVal/NumRec)*100

where:

NumVal = Number of valid hours of data received during the reporting period
NumRec = Number of hours of data received at STI during the reporting period.

The data recovery rate provides a method to evaluate the performance of the instruments.

As of the September 30, 1998 end of the first year of the project, data rates for June, July and August 1998 were available (and data for September 1998 were being processed).

The data recovery rates for the two sites for the high- mode winds are shown in Figure 3-3. The relatively low data recovery rates at low altitudes at the SMI site were attributed to interference from sea clutter. The VRM22D profiler installation was less sensitive to sea clutter and did not experience similar data losses.

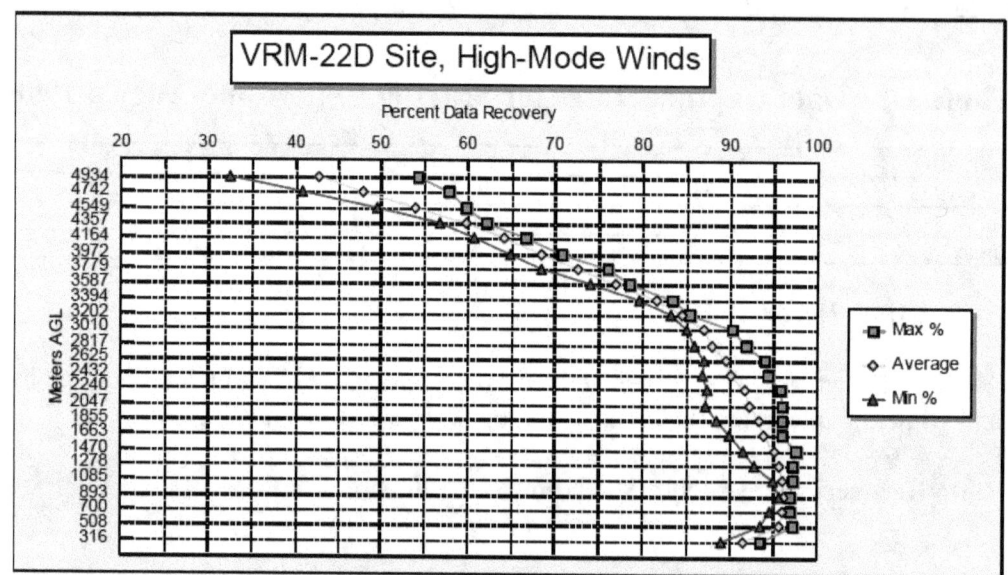

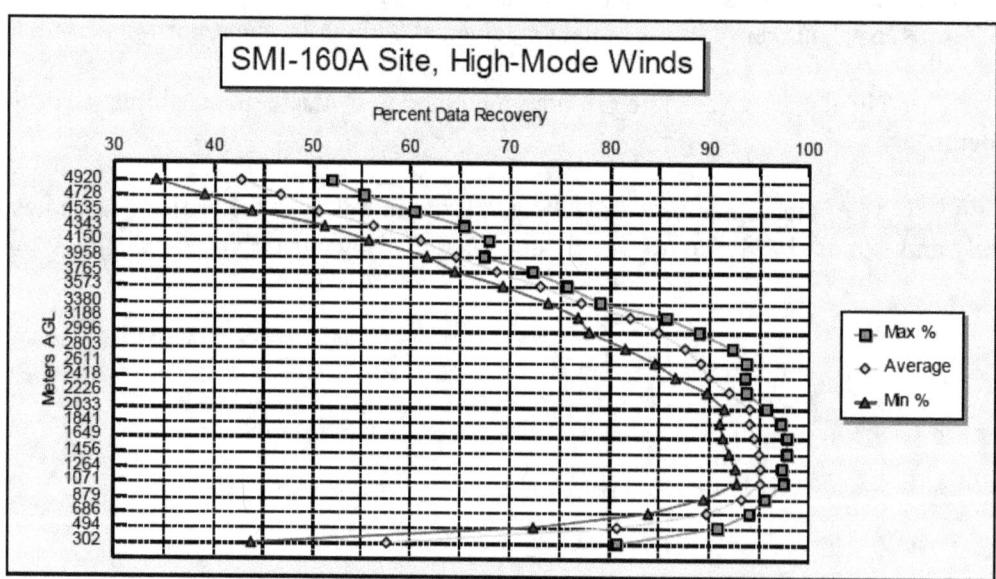

Figure 3-3. Data Recovery Rates for Radar Profiler High-Mode Winds, June-August 1998

The data recovery rates for the two sites for the low-mode winds are shown in Figure 3-4. Both sites experienced data recovery losses at the lowest altitudes due primarily to sea clutter interference.

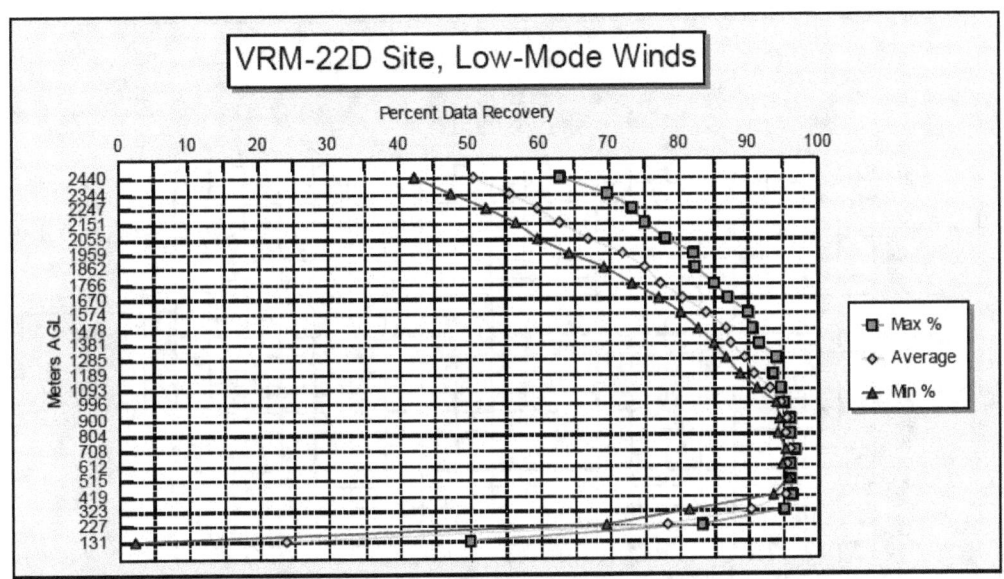

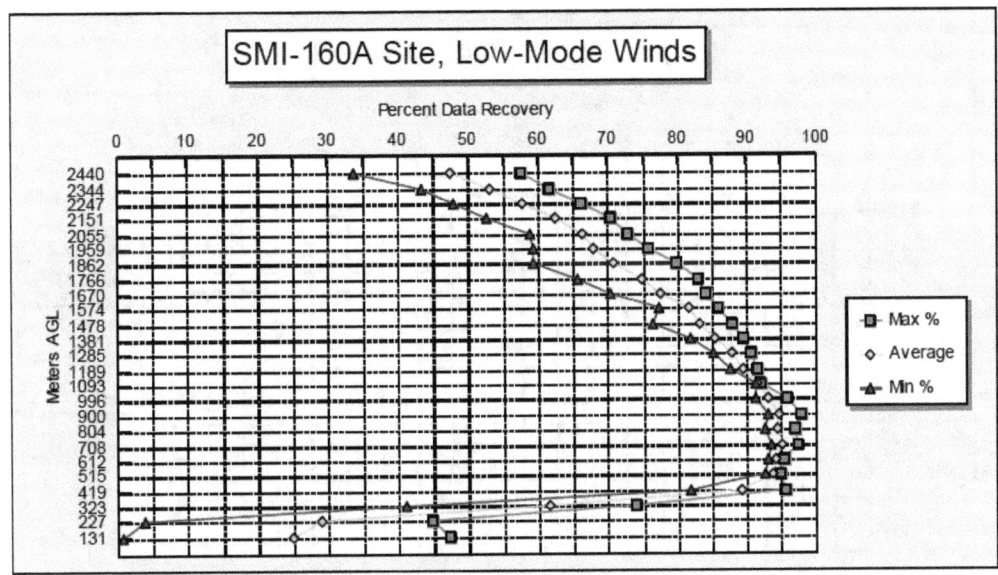

Figure 3-4. Data Recovery Rates for Radar Profiler Low-Mode Winds, June-August 1998

In the RASS mode, virtual temperature profiles are measured by using the scattering of radar pulses from acoustic waves. The data recovery rates for the radar profiler RASS mode are shown in Figure 3-5.

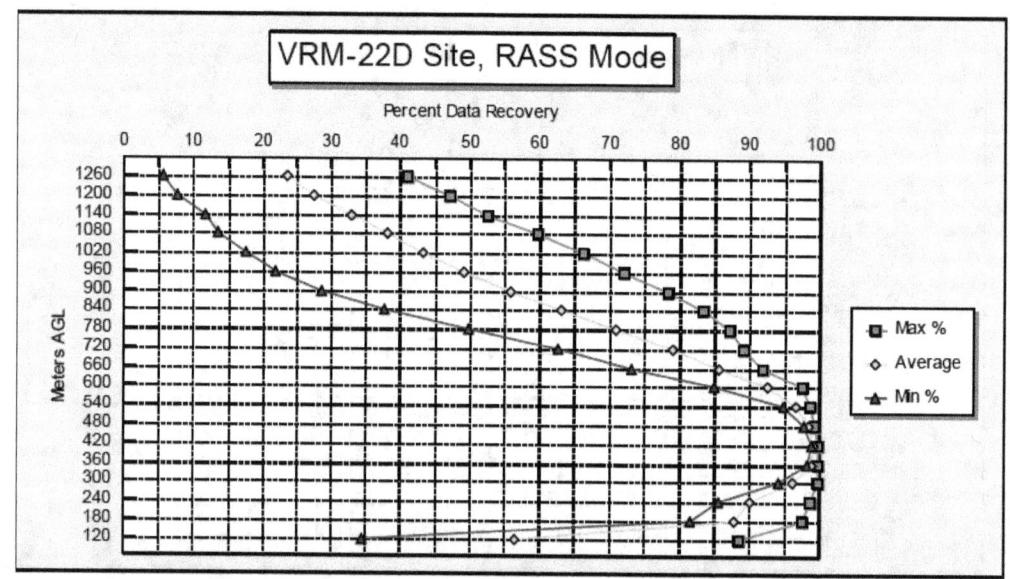

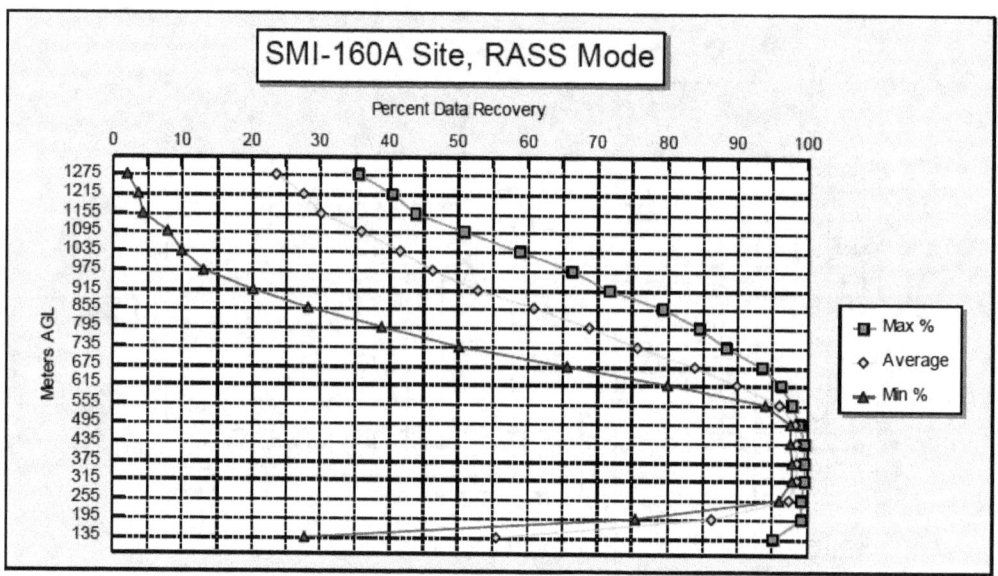

Figure 3-5. Data Recovery Rates for Radar Profiler RASS Mode, June-August 1998

RASS data losses at the lower altitudes during July and August were due to a configuration problem, and not due to clutter interference as in the wind modes. In the RASS mode, the acoustic source is programmed to sweep across a frequency band that corresponds to the range of expected atmospheric virtual temperatures. For the initial part of the collection period, the maximum temperature was set too low, resulting in lost data at low altitudes on hot days. During a site visit in September 1998, the parameter set was adjusted to cover a higher temperature range so that the lower altitude data would not be lost.

3.1.4.4   Examples of Wind and Temperature Profiles

Wind profiles for the high-mode winds at the South Marsh Island deep water site for August 28 are shown in Figure 3-6.

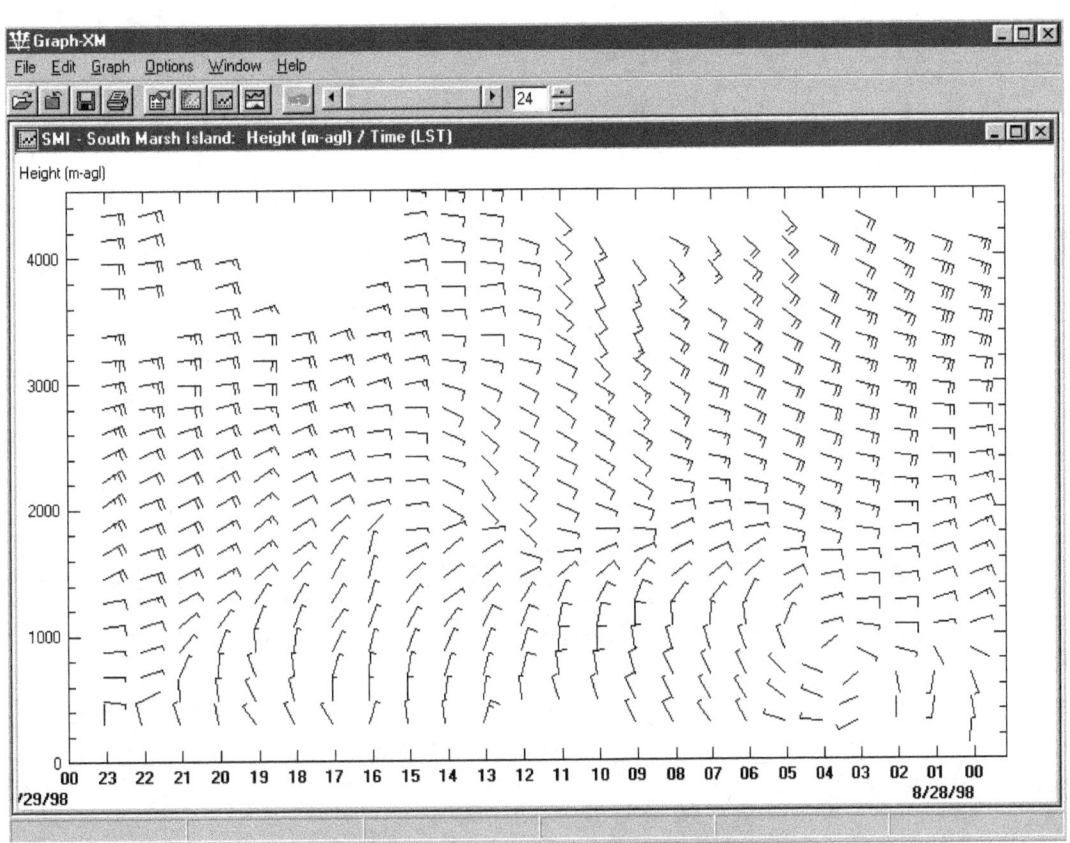

Figure 3-6. High-Mode Wind Profiles for SMI160A on August 28, 1998

Advancing time runs along the horizontal scale (x-axis from right to left). In this example, measured winds above approximately 2000 m were consistently from the east, whereas winds below that altitude show changing boundary layer conditions in detail.

Sample virtual temperature profiles measured by the radar profiler in the RASS mode at the Vermillion site on August 28 are shown in Figure 3-7.

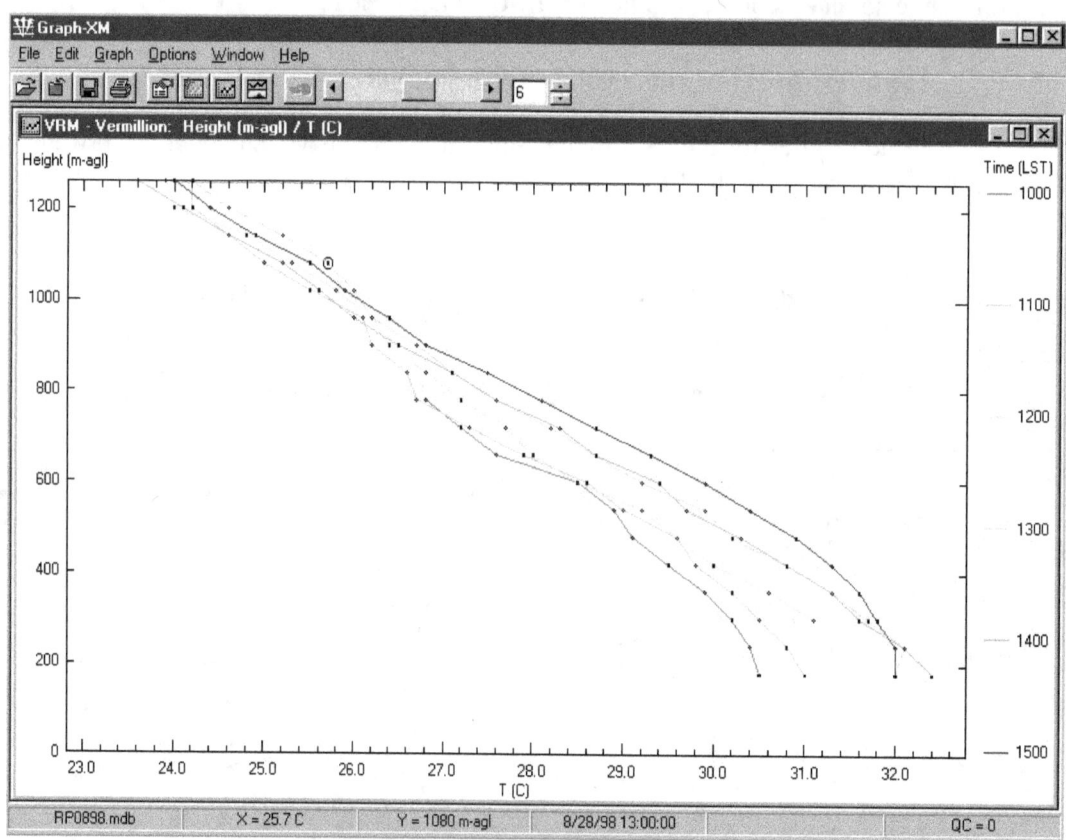

Figure 3-7. Virtual Temperature Profiles for VRM22D on August 28, 1998

The left-most temperature profile is at 10:00 am with right-most at 3:00 pm (15:00). This showed typical expected warming of the lower atmosphere into the day's heating cycle.

3.1.5   Problems Encountered and Corrective Action Taken

No problems involving the management of the project were experienced during the first year of the project.

Table 3-6 lists the equipment problems encountered, and the corrective action implemented, during the first year of the project.

Table 3-6. Project Year One Equipment Problems and Corrective Actions

Ref No.	Problem	Project Team Corrective Action
1-1	Long lead time for initial receipt of GOES DCP equipment and channel allocations.	Borrowed a GOES DCP and channel allocation from NOAA's Aeronomy Laboratory for use during the software development, testing, and integration prior to the start of the data collection period.
1-2	Delay in receiving RF broadcast licenses for the measurement sites. Government licenses were required for both sites to permit radar profiler operations (transmission of RF signals) and to permit RF communications up-link of the data from the sites to the GOES satellite.	Worked closely with all Government agencies involved to help move the process forward as quickly as possible. In spite of these efforts, the start of the data collection period was delayed from late March 1998 (at which time both sites had been installed and fully tested) until early June 1998 (at which time the RF licenses had been received and necessary site retesting to confirm operational readiness had been completed).
1-3	Failures of MMS-furnished temperature/RH sensors during initial systems integration and testing prior to site deployments.	MMS purchased two new sensors and provided them to the prime contractor as additional Government Furnished Equipment (GFE) in June 1998.
1-4	Poor telephone line quality to the selected platform sites. The digital links to the Gateway Computer at each site initially had high failure rate because of noise on the telephone lines.	Changed the communications software in use to connect to the Gateway Computer at each site from PC Anywhere to ProComm. It was determined that ProComm operated much more reliably in high noise conditions.
1-5	The circuit breakers controlling the platform-provided power to the radar profiler at VRM22D initially failed often because of high sensitivity to the "noisy" power on the platforms.	Replaced the circuit breakers with a more robust commercial model.
1-6	At VRM22D the RASS antennas had to be installed near the crew quarters. Noise generated by the antennas potentially interfered with crew sleep.	Reduced the audio amplifier transmit level to reduce the noise output of the antennas and the associated annoyance potential. Note: This necessarily also reduced RASS virtual temperature sensing height somewhat.
1-7	The GOES Data Collection Platform (DCP) failed at SMI160A during installation.	Replaced the failed GOES DCP unit with the project's spare, and returned the failed unit to Synergetics for repair.

Table 3-6.   Project Year One Equipment Problems and Corrective Actions (Cont'd)

Ref No.	Problem	Project Team Corrective Action
1-8	Sale of SMI160A by Chevron to Newfield Exploration in July 1998, one month after the start of the data collection period.	Obtained approval from the new owner to continue to use the platform as one of the two measurement sites for this MMS project. Also, after a prolonged negotiation period, secured Newfield agreement to waive their standard liability policy regarding platform access by project personnel to perform site equipment checks. As written, that policy was unacceptable to the prime contract for this MMS project because it would hold Newfield harmless for any injury to project personnel even if it were determined that negligence by Newfield had caused the injury.
1-9	RASS data recovery rates unexpectedly dropped during July and August 1998 and it was determined that the configuration settings in the radar profiler software needed to be further optimized for summer conditions in the Gulf (to increase the range of upper air temperatures that the RASS was set to measure).	Adjusted the configuration settings to implement the needed RASS temperature range increase. This was accomplished at both sites during the scheduled visits performed 9/14/98 – 9/17/98.
1-10	VRM22D and SMI160A were evacuated and the power was shut down at VRM22D for a 2 day period in early September 1998 due to Tropical Storm Earl. No upper air data were collected at VRM22D during this period, but surface met data at VRM22D continued to be collected since that portion of the equipment was able to continue to operate on battery power.	Worked with platform personnel to help assure the radar profiler was restored to operation at VRM22D as soon as possible after the tropical storm threat passed and power was restored at VRM22D. No tropical storm damage to project equipment was sustained at either site.
1-11	VRM22D and SMI160A were evacuated and the power was shut down on both platforms for a 4 day period in late September 1998 due to Hurricane Georges. No upper air data were collected during this period, but surface met data continued to be collected since that portion of the equipment was able to continue to operate on battery power.	Worked with platform personnel to help assure the radar profiler was restored to operation at each site as soon as possible after the hurricane passed and power was restored to the sites. No hurricane damage to project equipment at either site was sustained.

Table 3-6. Project Year One Equipment Problems and Corrective Actions (Cont'd)

Ref No.	Problem	Project Team Corrective Action
1-12	An SMI160A platform worker accidently broke the power switch on the GOES DCP while attempting to restore site operations on 9/29/98 after a 4-day platform power shutdown caused by Hurricane George.	Replaced the GOES DCP with the spare unit during an unscheduled visit to SMI160A on 10/10/98. Subsequently sent the failed unit to Synergetics for repair of the broken power switch.

3.1.6   Summary

Tasks completed during the first year of work on this project successfully supported project objectives. Site and equipment preparation were completed as planned, except that RF license applications took longer to process through the Department of Interior (requesting agency) and the NTIA (approving agency) than anticipated. Following receipt of the necessary RF licenses in late May 1998, the three year data collection period was initiated as of June 3, 1998. All data measurements collected were quality checked on a daily basis and were processed and documented by formal reporting on a monthly basis.

The project's data capture rate goal of 90% or greater was achieved during each of the first three data months.

3.2   Project Year Two Activities (10/01/98 - 09/30/99)

Work accomplished and results achieved during the second year of the project, October 1, 1998 through September 30, 1999, are detailed below.

3.2.1   Management

MMS and contractor participants continued to maintain a highly effective project team working relationship, using e-mail and telephone conferences to coordinate implementation actions and to resolve potential problems as they arose.

3.2.1.1   Personnel

Table 3-7 shows the key personnel participants in the project during the second year. Richard West replaced Carlton Schneider as the Prinicipal Engineer during the second year of the project.

Table 3-7. Project Year Two Key Personnel

Project Function	Person Performing Function	Comments
MMS Contracting Officer (CO)	Wally Adcox	
MMS Contracting Officer's Technical Representative (COTR)	Alex Lugo-Fernandez	
Program Manger	Gary Zeigler	Radian (later Vaisala)
Principal Investigator	Tim Dye	STI
Principal Engineer	Richard West	Radian (later Vaisala). Replaced Carlton Schneider

3.2.1.2   Communications and Coordination

Authority for all required project team decision actions to ensure timely, efficient, and competent accomplishment of all work under the contract continued to be vested in the Program Manager. Authority for day-to-day decision making continued to be delegated to the Principal Engineer for all equipment-related matters and to the Principal Investigator for all data collection and processing matters.

Routine meetings necessary for smooth implementations of the measurement sites were replaced with as-needed teleconferences.

All formal external communications and coordination by project team members continued to be directed through the Program Manager. Informal communications and coordinating with personnel and agencies outside the project team were encouraged by individual team members as necessary to ensure effective accomplishment of the routine work within the responsibility of the respective team participant. Issues that arose during such informal external contacts were immediately reported through the project management chain to the Program Manager for formal resolution.

3.2.1.3 Record Keeping

The project contract file, including copies of all correspondence with the MMS Contracting Officer, continued to be maintained in the office of the Contract Specialist.

A copy of all documentation related to project accomplishment continued to be maintained in the office of the Program Manager. These documents include all project directives, reports of trips and meetings, record copies of all written deliverables submitted to MMS, and copies of all written correspondence between the Program Manager and the MMS COTR.

Data collection and processing, chain of custody, and other quality assurance records continued to be maintained by the Principal Investigator. These records serve as the basis of monthly and annual reporting, as well as other formal submissions.

Equipment testing, installation, operation, maintenance, and quality assurance records continued to be maintained by the Principal Engineer. The Principal Engineer also continued to maintain a log of all scheduled and unscheduled site visit activities and the results thereof. These records serve as the basis of monthly and annual reporting, as well as other formal submissions, that were initiated by the Principal Engineer, through the Program Manager, to MMS as contract deliverables.

Photographic records of all significant project activities continued to be taken by project team members, under the direction of project key personnel, as inputs to MMS under the "Presentation Slide Sets" deliverable requirement of the contract.

3.2.2 Site and Equipment Preparation Logistics

3.2.2.1 Site Selection

Details on the original site-finding efforts and results are described in Section 3.1.2.1 of this report. To recap, the following two platforms were selected for the study:

1) Vermillion 22D, operated by ERT, as the shallow water site; and

2) South Marsh Island 160A, originally operated by Chevron, and subsequently by Newfield Exploration, as the deep water site.

3.2.2.2   RF Licenses

As described in Section 3.1.2.2 of this report, RF licenses were required (and obtained) for the GOES satellite data up-link and for the wind profiler operating frequency.

- The profiler data were transmitted using a two-minute per hour channel of the NOAA/NESDIS Geostationary Operational Environmental Satellite (GOES) system. Allocation of the channel from NESDIS and permitting from NTIA to transmit to the GOES satellite at 402 MHz were required and received.

- The wind profiler measurements were based on radar pulses centered at 915 MHz. Permission from NTIA to operate the two profilers in the Gulf of Mexico in this band was required and received.

There were no problems with our licenses during the second year of the project.

3.2.2.3   Equipment

During the second year of the project, there were no changes to the measurement equipment used at the two sites, as previously listed in Table 3-2, except that lens-protecting tubes were added to the sea surface temperature sensors as described in Table 3-11, reference number 2-3.

3.2.2.4   Data Processing

The data processing and communications tasks continued to include include preparing the data at the sites, transmitting the data back through GOES, receiving the data at the STI Weather Operations Center, analyzing and storing the data, and submitting data reports.

During the second year of the project, no procedure or data flow changes were needed or made. There were some problems with real-time data collection due to GOES DCP and platform power disruptions, but all were addressed in timely fashion to keep capture rates high.

3.2.3   Site Operations and Maintenance

During the second year of the project, two scheduled site visits and three unscheduled visits were performed, as listed in Table 3-8.

Table 3-8. Project Year Two Site Visits

Visit Date	Site(s) Visited	Visit Type	Visit Tasks Completed
10/9/98 – 10/10/98	VRM22D & SMI160A	Unscheduled	At VRM22D, replaced SST sensor that failed 10/1/98.
			At SMI160A, installed spare GOES DCP (replacing unit with power switch that was accidently broken by platform personnel during their platform power shutdown for Hurricane Georges).
12/17/98	VRM22D	Unscheduled	Replaced SST sensor that failed 11/2/98
			As precaution, also replaced RH sensor because data starting to become suspect
4/20/99	VRM22D & SMI160A	Scheduled	Performed periodic equipment audits
			At SMI160A, replaced corroded SST sensor.
8/6/99 – 8/7/99	VRM22D	Unscheduled	Repaired radar profiler and restored GOES transmission of upper air data following a lightning strike on 8/3/99. Attempted unsuccessfully to restore GOES transmission of surface met data. Confirmed surface met data being recorded at the site, however, so planned further repair to restore GOES surface met data transmission during next scheduled site visit.
9/29/99 – 9/30/99	VRM22D & SMI160A	Scheduled	Performed periodic equipment audits
			At VRM22D, repaired connection between the data logger and Gateway computer (damaged by 8/3/99 lightning strike) and restored GOES surface met data transmission. As precautions, also added surge protectors on the serial line between the data logger and Gateway Computer, and replaced the short-haul modem with direct RS-232 connection to improve met data transfer. Replaced the temp/RH and SST sensors (due to audit results).
			At SMI160A, added precautionary surge protectors on the serial line between the data logger and Gateway computer. Restored GOES transmissions by clearing a Gateway Computer interrupt. Also removed a failed UPS unit and made arrangements to have platform personnel ship it to Vaisala for repair.

3.2.4   Data Measurements

3.2.4.1   Description

The Gateway computer on each platform continued to collect data from the radar profiler, the surface meteorological instrument datalogger, and the GPS receiver. Once each hour, the latest data continued to be packed into a compressed format and transmitted through the GOES satellite link to a database on the NOAA/NESDIS system in Wallops Island, VA.

Automated procedures in the STI weather operations facility continued to be used to retrieve and unpack the data files. The STI staff continued to review the data daily to ensure that all of the collection systems were operating correctly. At the end of each month, the prior month's data continued to be processed to quality-stamp any suspect and invalid measurements. A monthly data report is then generated. The validated monthly data also continued to be loaded into a database archive.

3.2.4.2   Data Capture Rate

The data capture rate measures the up-time of the integrated data collection and communications systems at each site. It is defined using:

Data Capture Rate = (NumRec/NumPos)*100

where:

NumRec = number of hours of data received at STI during the reporting period
NumPos = number of hours of data possible during the reporting period
         (for example, 30 x 24 = 720 in a 30 day reporting period)

As of the September 30, 1999 end of the second year of the project, data rates for September 1998 through August 1999 were available (and data for September 1999 were being processed). The data capture rates for September 1998 through August 1999 from the VRM22D site are shown in Table 3-9, and from the SMI160A site in Table 3-10. The goal of the MMS program was to achieve a capture rate of 90% or higher. The actual average data capture rate for all sensors for the September 1998-August 1999 collection period was 92.4%. The capture rate for the total program through August 1999 was 93.4%.

**Table 3-9. Data Capture Rates for VRM22D Site,
September 1998-August 1999**

Date	Upper Air Winds	Upper Air T_v	Surface Met
Sep-98	80.7%	81.0%	100%
Oct-98	95.2%	95.3%	95.3%
Nov-98	96.8%	96.7%	96.9%
Dec-98	97.3%	97.3%	97.3%
Jan-99	94.2%	94.2%	94.2%
Feb-99	97.6%	97.6%	97.6%
Mar-99	95.4%	95.4%	95.8%
Apr-99	74.4%	74.4%	71.9%
May-99	97.9%	97.9%	98.7%
Jun-99	72.8%	72.6%	72.4%
Jul-99	98.8%	91.8%	98.8%
Aug-99	87.0%	78.4%	8.7%
Annual Average	90.7%	89.4%	85.6%

**Table 3-10. Data Capture Rates for SMI160A Site,
September 1998-August 1999**

Date	Upper Air Winds	Upper Air T_v	Surface Met
Sep-98	85.3%	85.5%	100%
Oct-98	90.7%	91.0%	87.6%
Nov-98	98.9%	98.8%	99.0%
Dec-98	87.5%	87.4%	94.8%
Jan-99	99.5%	99.5%	99.5%
Feb-99	96.1%	96.1%	96.1%
Mar-99	97.7%	97.7%	98.1%
Apr-99	98.9%	99.0%	99.3%
May-99	98.5%	98.5%	99.3%
Jun-99	98.1%	98.1%	98.1%
Jul-99	97.9%	97.9%	97.9%
Aug-99	99.3%	99.5%	99.5%
Annual Average	95.7%	95.8%	97.4%

3.2.4.3   Data Recovery Rate

The data recovery rate is defined as the percentage of valid data captured by each instrument while the integrated system is operational. It is calculated using:

Data Recovery Rate = (NumVal/NumRec)*100

where:

NumVal = Number of valid hours of data received during the reporting period
NumRec = Number of hours of data received at STI during the reporting period.
The data recovery rate provides a method to evaluate the performance of the instruments.

As of the September 30, 1999 end date of the second year of the project, data rates for September 1998 through August 1999 were available (and data for September 1999 were being processed). These figures illustrate data capture rate for each site in a series of graphs that are labeled "Max %", "Average", and "Min %". The graphs are, respectively:

The maximum monthly capture rate over the twelve months in the sample;
The average monthly capture rate over the twelve months in the sample;
The minimum monthly capture rate over the twelve months in the sample.

The horizontal (or x) scale is the percent of data capture and the vertical (or y) scale is the measurement altitude in meters AGL.

3.2.4.3.1   Radar Profiler High-Mode Wind Data

The data recovery rates for the two sites for the high-mode winds are shown in Figure 3-8. The relatively low data recovery rates at low altitudes at the SMI site were attributed to interference from sea clutter. The VRM profiler installation is less sensitive to sea clutter and did not experience similar data losses.

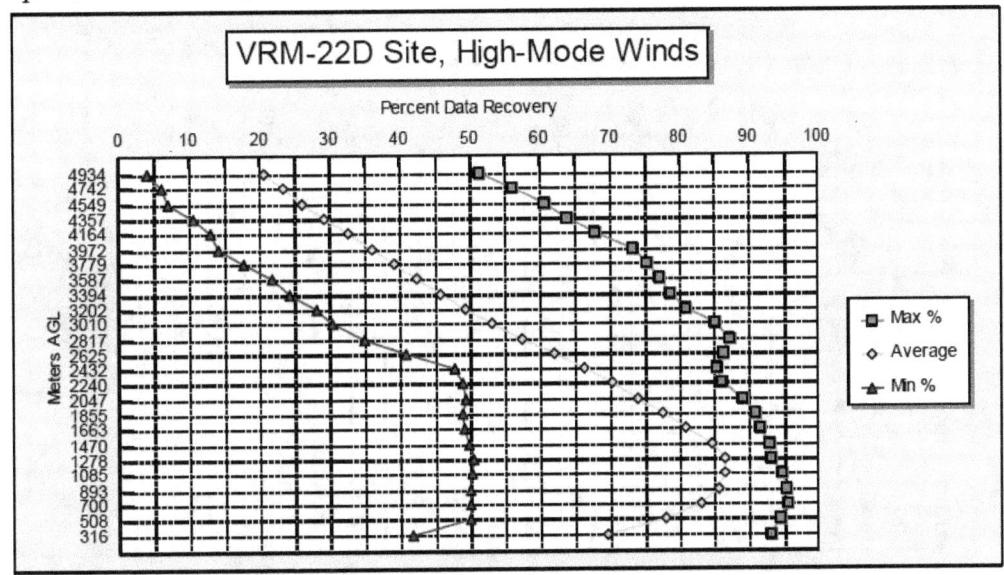

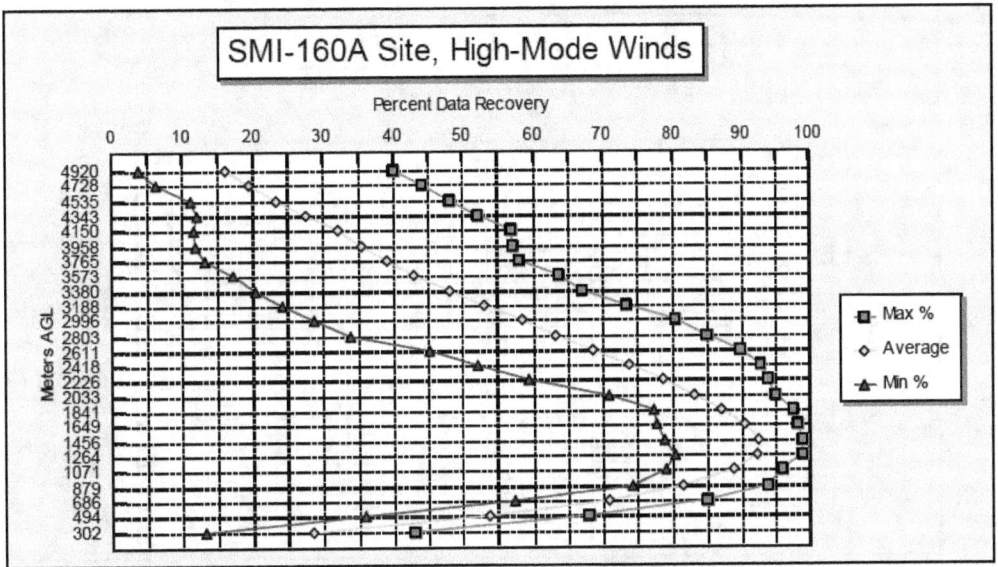

Figure 3-8. Data Recovery Rates for Radar Profiler High-Mode Winds, September 1998 - August 1999

3.2.4.3.2 Radar Profiler Low-Mode Wind Data

The data recovery rates for the two sites for low-mode winds are shown in Figure 3-9. Both sites experienced data recovery losses at the lowest altitudes due primarily to sea clutter interference.

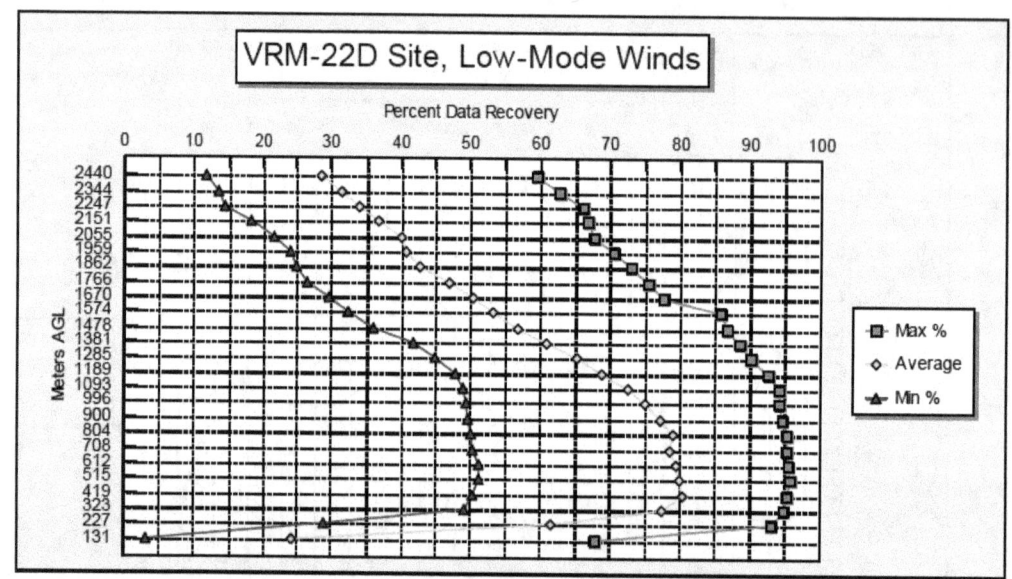

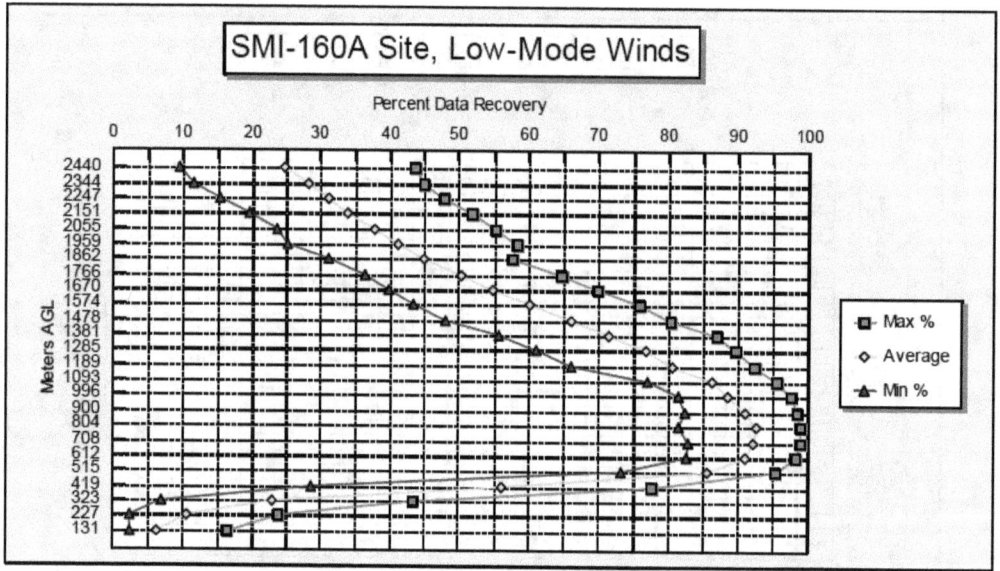

Figure 3-9. Data Recovery Rates for Radar Profiler Low-Mode Winds, September 1998 - August 1999

3.2.4.3.3   RASS Temperature Data

In the RASS mode, virtual temperature profiles are measured by using the scattering of radar pulses from acoustic waves. The data recovery rates for the radar profiler RASS mode are shown in Figure 3-10.

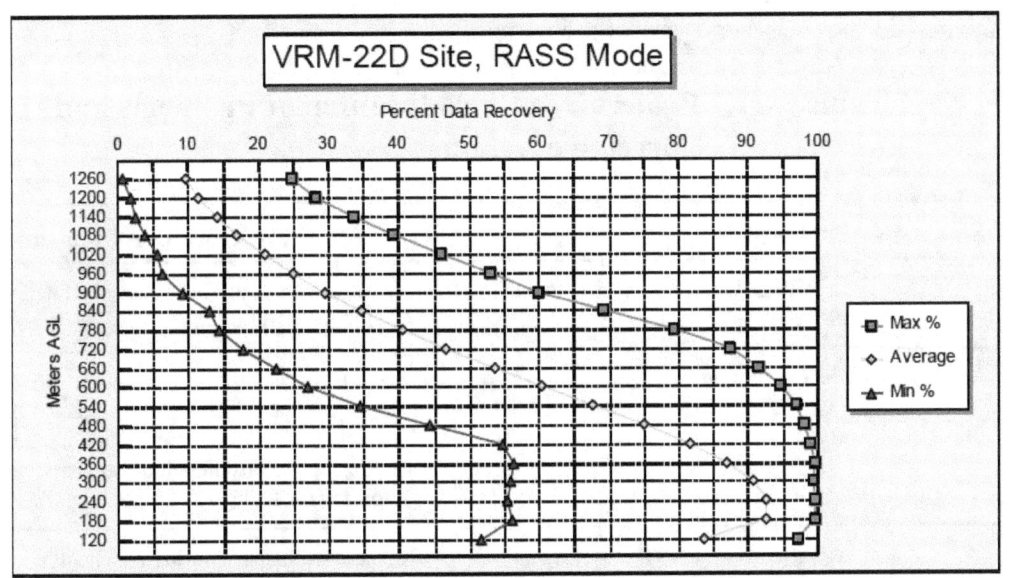

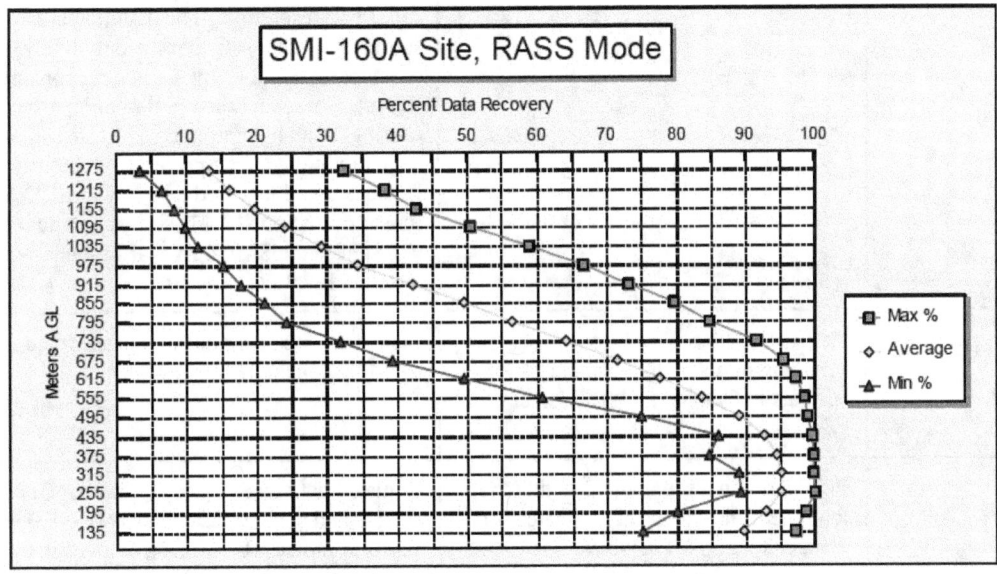

**Figure 3-10. Data Recovery Rates for Radar Profiler RASS Mode,
September 1998 - August 1999**

3.2.5   Problems Encountered and Corrective Action Taken

No problems involving the management of the project were experienced during the second year of the project.

Table 3-11 lists the equipment problems encountered, and the corrective action implemented during the second year of the project.

Table 3-11.   Project Year Two Equipment Problems and Corrective Actions

Ref No.	Problem	Project Team Corrective Action
2-1	At VRM22D the SST sensor failed on 10/1/98.	Replaced with spare during unscheduled visit to VRM22D on 10/10/98.
2-2	The GOES transmission system was inoperative for 18 hours on 10/27/98.	The GOES systems was restored by NESDIS. The project team retrieved the collected data during this period from the computers at the sites during the unscheduled site visits performed on 12/17/98.
2-3	At VRM22D the SST sensor again failed on 11/2/98.	Replaced with spare during unscheduled visit to VRM22D on 12/17/98. Also worked with the SST manufacturer to attempt to identify failure cause and resolution. The manufacturer subsequently advised that the only likely problem is that the lens was being contaminated with sea spray and then giving unrepresentative readings. In an attempt to reduce sea spray contamination, a lens-protecting tube was fabricated and installed on the VRM22D SST sensor during our 12/17/98. An identical tube was sent to the SMI160A platform and was installed by platform personnel.
2-4	At VRM22D the RH sensor began providing periodically unstable readings in October and November 1998.	Replaced with spare during unscheduled visit to VRM22D on 12/17/98.
2-5	Discovered in December 1998 that the computer time stamps at both sites had changed to CDT. They have been configured to remain on CST.	Adjusted data taken since the start of CDT back to CST and sent replacement (corrected) data to MMS in January 1999. Began investigating cause of the problem, but no immediate conclusions were reached.

Table 3-11. Project Year Two Equipment Problems and Corrective Actions (Cont'd)

Ref No.	Problem	Project Team Corrective Action
2-6	At VRM22D the computers started having problems keeping track of time as of 4/10/99.	Resolved by remote connection to the VRM22D computer and with the help of platform personnel. Cause appeared to be platform power instability, which apparently caused the problem when power was lost during a GPS clock update to the computer. Took five days to resolve because of the complexity of the problem and time lost awaiting platform power and personnel availability.
2-7	At VRM22D the GOES transmitter was found to be unreliable (and was considered failed) during the scheduled 4/20/99 visit to that site. At SMI160A the SST sensor was found to be highly corroded during the scheduled 4/20/99 visit to that site.	Replaced the GOES transmitter with spare during the 4/20/99 site visit. Replaced the SST sensor with spare during the 4/20/99 site visit.
2-8	At VRM22D the GOES transmissions began having software interrupt problems on 6/15/99.	Resolved on 6/23/99 by remote connection to the VRM22D computer and with the help of platform personnel. This fix was delayed by a platform telephone outage and awaiting availability of platform personnel to assist.
2-9	The VRM22D platform sustained a direct lightning strike on 8/3/99, stopping all project met equipment operation.	Repaired the radar profiler and restored GOES transmission of upper air data from VRM22D during an unscheduled visit to the platform on 8/6/99 and 8/7/99. Attempted unsuccessfully to restore GOES transmission of surface met data during this visit, but did confirm the data were being collected and therefore deferred further action until the next scheduled platform visit in September 1999. On 9/29/99 repaired the connection between the data logger and Gateway Computer at VRM22D, restoring GOES transmission of surface met data. Also installed additional surge protection at both VRM22D and SMI160A during this visit to attempt to prevent recurrence due to future lightning strikes.
2-10	At VRM22D the temperature/RH sensor and the SST sensors failed audit criteria during the 9/29/99 site visit.	Replaced both sensors during the visit.

Table 3-11. Project Year Two Equipment Problems and Corrective Actions (Cont'd)

Ref No.	Problem	Project Team Corrective Action
2-11	At SMI160A the UPS unit was found to have an internal battery problem during the 9/30/99 site visit.	Removed the UPS unit and shipped it for repair. This UPS unit was subsequently repaired and was reinstalled at SMI160A during a scheduled site visit in June 2000.

3.2.6 Summary

Tasks completed during the second year of work on this project successfully supported the objective. Sites and equipment were rigorously monitored, problems quickly addressed, and reports submitted on time. All data measurements collected were quality checked on a daily basis and were processed and documented by formal reporting on a monthly basis.

During the second year of the project, the average data capture rate was 92.4%, which met the project's 90% or higher goal. As of the end of the second year of the project, the cumulative data capture rate for the project was 93.4%, which also met the project's 90% or higher goal.

3.3 Project Year Three Activities (10/01/99 - 09/30/00)

Work accomplished and results achieved during the third year of the project, October 1, 1999 through September 30, 2000, are detailed below.

3.3.1 Management

MMS and contractor participants continued to maintain a highly effective project team working relationship, using e-mail and telephone conferences to coordinate and to resolve potential problems as they arose.

3.3.1.1 Personnel

Table 3-12 shows the key personnel participants in the project during the third year. Dr. Chester Huang replaced Dr. Alex Lugo-Fernandez as COTR and Bill Burton replaced Richard West as Principal Engineer.

Table 3-12. Project Year Three Key Personnel

Project Function	Person Performing Function	Comments
MMS Contracting Officer (CO)	Wally Adcox	
MMS Contracting Officer's Technical Representative (COTR)	Chester Huang	Replaced Alex Lugo-Fernandez
Program Manger	Gary Zeigler	Radian (later Vaisala)
Principal Investigator	Tim Dye	STI
Principal Engineer	Bill Burton	Radian (later Vaisala). Replaced Richard West

3.3.1.2   Communications and Coordination

Authority for all required project team decision actions to ensure timely, efficient, and competent accomplishment of all work under the contract continued to be vested in the Program Manager. Authority for day-to-day decision making continued to be delegated to the Principal Engineer for all equipment-related matters and to the Principal Investigator for all data collection and processing matters.

Routine meetings were conducted by as-needed teleconferences.

All formal external communications and coordination by project team members continued to be directed through the Program Manager. Informal communications and coordinating with personnel and agencies outside the project team were encouraged by individual team members as necessary to ensure effective accomplishment of the routine work within the responsibility of the respective team participant. Issues that arose during such informal external contacts were immediately reported through the project management chain to the Program Manager for formal resolution.

3.3.1.3   Record Keeping

The project contract file, including copies of all correspondence with the MMS Contracting Officer, continued to be maintained in the office of the Contract Specialist.

A copy of all documentation related to project accomplishment continued to be maintained in the office of the Program Manager. These documents include all project directives, reports of trips and meetings, record copies of all written deliverables submitted to MMS, and copies of all written correspondence between the Program Manager and the MMS COTR.

Data collection and processing, chain of custody, and other quality assurance records continued to be maintained by the Principal Investigator. These records serve as the basis of monthly and annual reporting, as well as other formal submissions.

Equipment testing, installation, operation, maintenance, and quality assurance records continued to be maintained by the Principal Engineer. The Principal Engineer also continued to maintain a log of all scheduled and unscheduled site visit activities and the results thereof. These records serve as the basis of monthly and annual reporting, as well as other formal submissions, that were initiated by the Principal Engineer, through the Program Manager, to MMS as contract deliverables.

Photographic records of all significant project activities continued to be taken by project team members, under the direction of project key personnel, as inputs to MMS under the "Presentation Slide Sets" deliverable requirement of the contract.

3.3.2 Site and Equipment Preparation Logistics

3.3.2.1 Site Selection

Details on the original site-finding efforts and results are described in Section 3.1.2.1 of this report. To recap, the following two platforms were selected for the study:

1) Vermillion 22D, operated by ERT, as the shallow water site; and

2) South Marsh Island 160A, originally operated by Chevron, and subsequently by Newfield Exploration, as the deep water site.

3.3.2.2 RF Licenses

As described in Section 3.1.2.2 of this report, RF licenses were required (and obtained) for the GOES satellite data up-link and for the wind profiler operating frequency.

- The profiler data were transmitted using a two-minute per hour channel of the NOAA/NESDIS Geostationary Operational Environmental Satellite (GOES) system. Allocation of the channel from NESDIS and permitting from NTIA to transmit to the GOES satellite at 402 MHz were required and received.

- The wind profiler measurements were based on radar pulses centered at 915 MHz. Permission from NTIA to operate the two profilers in the Gulf of Mexico in this band was required and received.

There were no problems with our licenses during the third year of the project.

3.3.2.3 Equipment

During the third year of the project, there were no changes to the measurement equipment used at the two sites, as previously listed in Table 3-2.

3.3.2.4　Data Processing

The data processing and communications tasks continued to include preparing the data at the sites, transmitting the data back through GOES, receiving the data at the STI Weather Operations Center, analyzing and storing the data, and submitting data reports.

During the third year of the project, no procedure or data flow changes were needed or made.

3.3.3　Site Operations and Maintenance

During the third year of the project, one scheduled site visit and two unscheduled visits were performed, as listed in Table 3-13.

Table 3-13. Project Year Three Site Visits

Visit Date	Site(s) Visited	Visit Type	Visit Tasks Completed
1/14/00 – 1/16/00	VRM22D & SMI160A	Unscheduled	At both sites, corrected a GPS problem that had caused the radar profilers to cease operations on 1/1/00 because the computers were being told the year was 1900 rather than 2000.
			Performed periodic equipment audits
3/24/00 – 3/26/00	VRM22D & SMI160A	Unscheduled	At VRM22D, replaced a failed power supply in the charger for the data logger and restored GOES transmissions of surface met data that had ceased on 2/26/00. Also at VRM22D, as a precaution (because of possible performance degradation), replaced the radar profiler's final amplifier
			At both sites, installed a software patch to help prevent potential future leap year problems.
6/14/00 – 6/16/00	VMR22D & SMI160A	Scheduled	Performed periodic equipment audits
			At both sites, also installed a Windows 95 patch to keep time stamps at CST all year
			At VRM22D, replaced the temp/RH sensor (due to audit results). Also restored GOES transmissions by clearing a Gateway Computer interrupt..
			At SMI160A, replaced temp/RH and SST sensors (due to audit results). Also installed repaired UPS unit.

3.3.4   Data Measurements

3.3.4.1   Description

The Gateway computer on each platform continued to collect data from the radar profiler, the surface meteorological instrument datalogger, and the GPS receiver. Once each hour, the latest data continued to be packed into a compressed format and transmitted through the GOES satellite link to a database on the NOAA/NESDIS system in Wallops Island, VA.

Automated procedures in the STI weather operations facility continued to be used to retrieve and unpack the data files. The STI staff continued to review the data daily to ensure that all of the collection systems were operating correctly. At the end of each month, the prior month's data continued to be processed to quality-stamp any suspect and invalid measurements. A monthly data report was then generated. The validated monthly data also continued to be loaded into a database archive.

3.3.4.2 Data Capture Rate

The data capture rate measures the up-time of the integrated data collection and communications systems at each site. It is defined using:

Data Capture Rate = (NumRec/NumPos)*100
where:
NumRec = number of hours of data received at STI during the reporting period
NumPos = number of hours of data possible during the reporting period

As of the September 30, 2000 end of the third year of the project, data rates for September 1999 through August 2000 were available (and data for September 2000 were being processed). The data capture rates for September 1999 through August 2000 from the VRM22D site are shown in Table 3-14, and from the SMI160A site in Table 3-15. The goal of the MMS program was to achieve a capture rate of 90% or higher. The actual average capture rate for all sensors for the September 1999-August 2000 collection period was 86.9%. The capture rate for the total program through August 2000 was 90.5%.

Table 3-14. Data Capture Rates for VRM22D Site, September 1999-August 2000

Date	Upper Air Winds	Upper Air T$_v$	Surface Met
Sep-99	96.7%	96.7%	1.4%
Oct-99	95.8%	95.7%	96.8%
Nov-99	96.5%	96.5%	96.4%
Dec-99	90.5%	90.3%	90.6%
Jan-00	49.9%	49.7%	94.5%
Feb-00	93.7%	93.7%	84.2%
Mar-00	60.2%	60.1%	23.7%
Apr-00	99.9%	99.9%	99.9%
May-00	98.9%	98.5%	100%
Jun-00	76.1%	59.0%	96.4%
Jul-00	98.0%	98.0%	98.0%
Aug-00	99.9%	99.9%	99.9%
Annual Average	88.0%	86.5%	85.2%

Table 3-15.   Data Capture Rates for SMI160A Site, September 1999-August 2000

Date	Upper Air Winds	Upper Air T$_v$	Surface Met
Sep-99	79.4%	79.4%	76.0%
Oct-99	69.5%	69.4%	83.7%
Nov-99	99.2%	99.2%	99.2%
Dec-99	94.2%	94.1%	97.7%
Jan-00	38.2%	40.5%	62.9%
Feb-00	96.8%	96.8%	97.0%
Mar-00	98.5%	98.5%	98.5%
Apr-00	95.0%	94.9%	95.0%
May-00	96.1%	96.2%	97.3%
Jun-00	97.1%	96.8%	96.4%
Jul-00	92.7%	92.6%	92.7%
Aug-00	90.5%	90.5%	90.5%
Annual Average	87.3%	87.1%	90.6%

3.3.4.3   Data Recovery

The data recovery rate is defined as the percentage of valid data captured by each instrument while the integrated system is operational. It is calculated using:

Data Recovery Rate = (NumVal/NumRec)*100

where:

NumVal = Number of valid hours of data received during the reporting period
NumRec = Number of hours of data received at STI during the reporting period.

The data recovery rate provides a method to evaluate the performance of the instruments.

As of the September 30, 2000 end of the third year of the project, data rates for September 1999 through August 2000 were available (and data for September 2000 were being processed). These figures illustrate data capture rate for each site in a series of graphs that are labeled "Max %", "Average", and "Min %". The graphs are, respectively:

The maximum monthly capture rate over the twelve months in the sample;
The average monthly capture rate over the twelve months in the sample;
The minimum monthly capture rate over the twelve months in the sample.

The horizontal (or x) scale is the percent of data capture and the vertical (or y) scale is the measurement altitude in meters AGL.

3.3.4.3.1   Radar Profiler High-Mode Wind Data

The data recovery rates for the two sites for the high-mode winds are shown in Figure 3-11. The relatively low data recovery rates at low altitudes at the SMI site were attributed to interference from sea clutter. The VRM profiler installation is less sensitive to sea clutter and did not experience similar data losses.

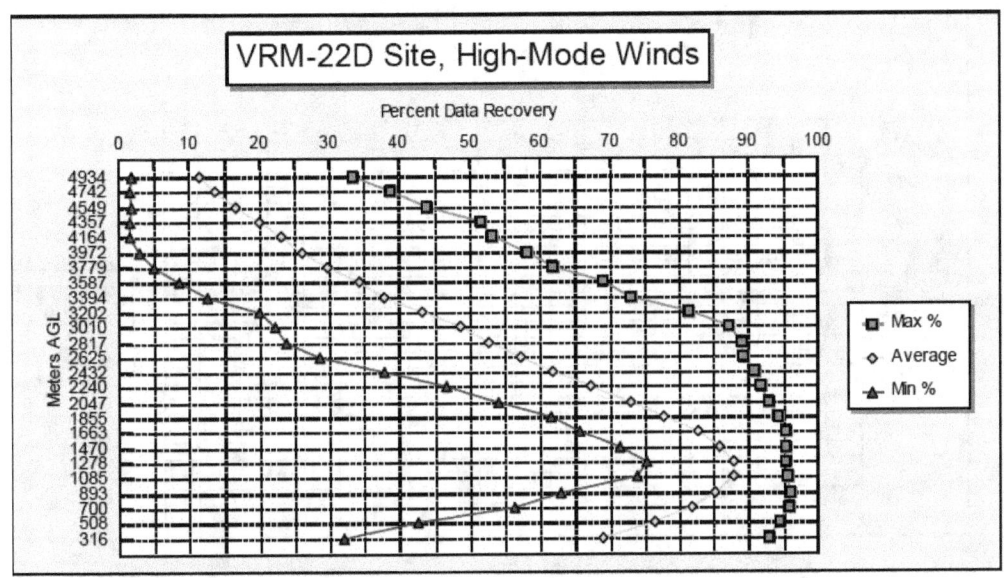

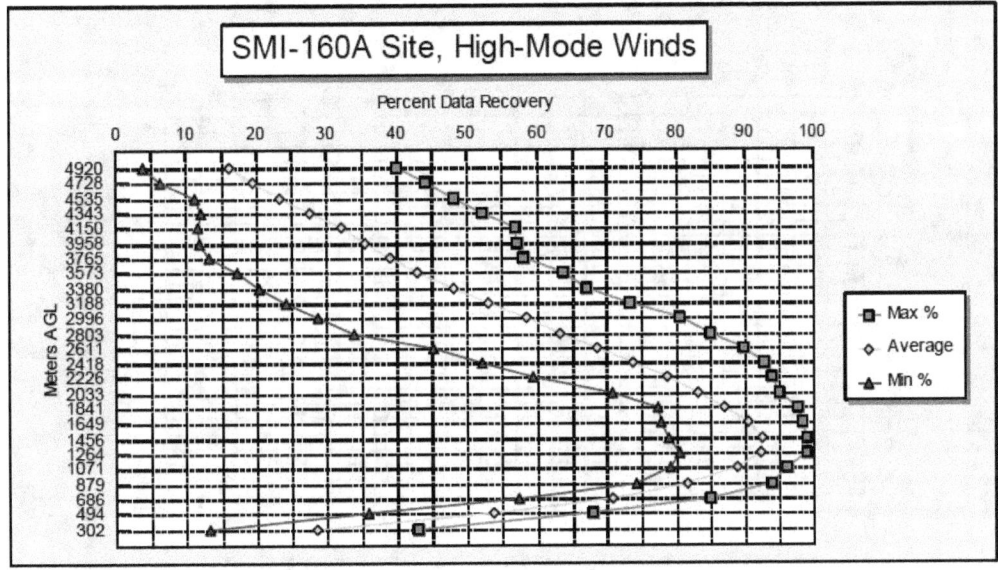

Figure 3-11. Data Recovery Rates for Radar Profiler High-Mode Winds, September 1999 - August 2000

3.3.4.3.2   Radar Profiler Low-Mode Wind Data

The data recovery rates for the two sites for low-mode winds are shown in Figure 3-12. Both sites experienced data recovery losses at the lowest altitudes due primarily to sea clutter interference.

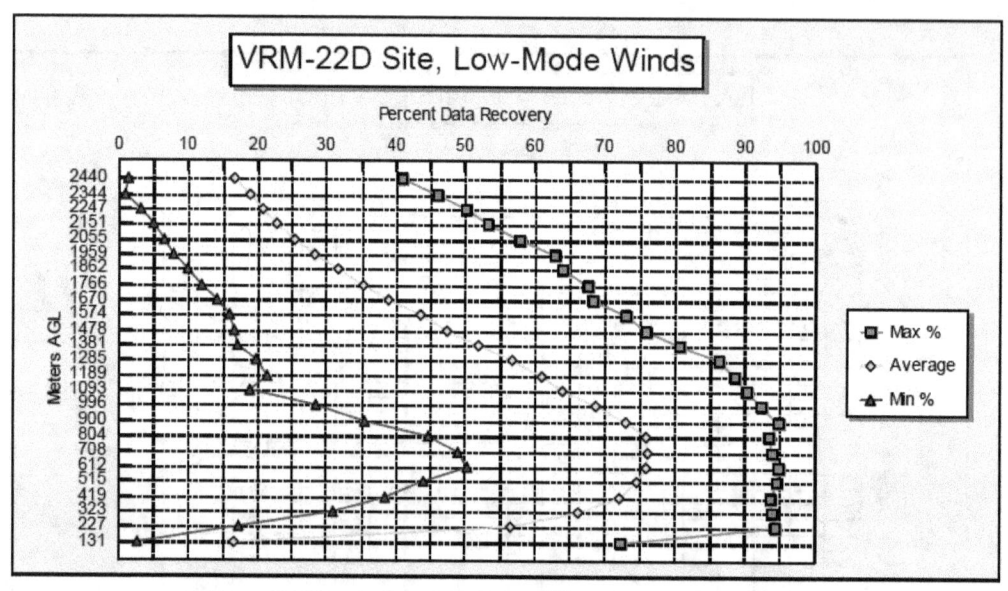

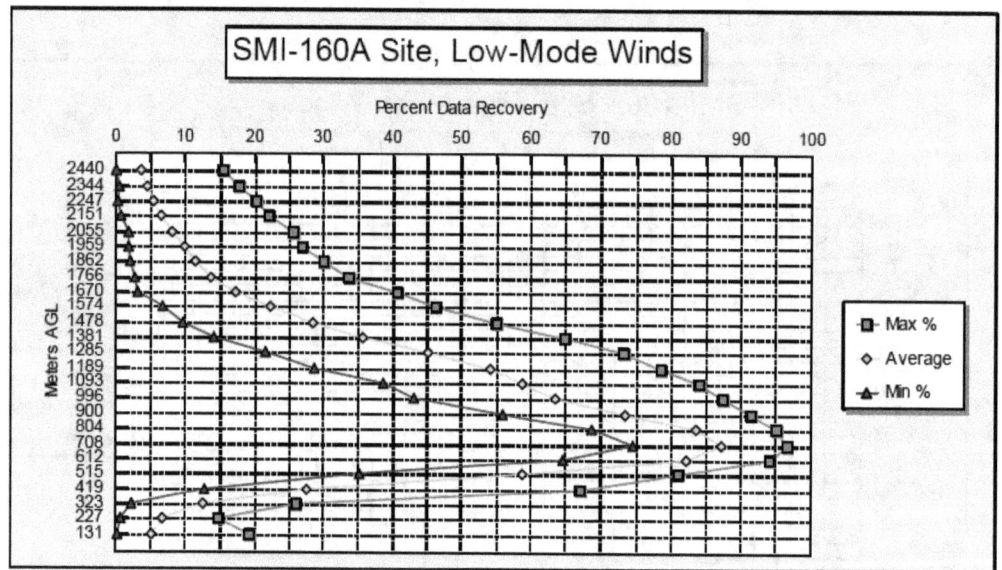

Figure 3-12. Data Recovery Rates for Radar Profiler Low-Mode Winds, September 1999 - August 2000

3.3.4.3.3   RASS Temperature Data

In the RASS mode, virtual temperature profiles are measured by using the scattering of radar pulses from acoustic waves. The data recovery rates for the radar profiler RASS mode are shown in Figure 3-13.

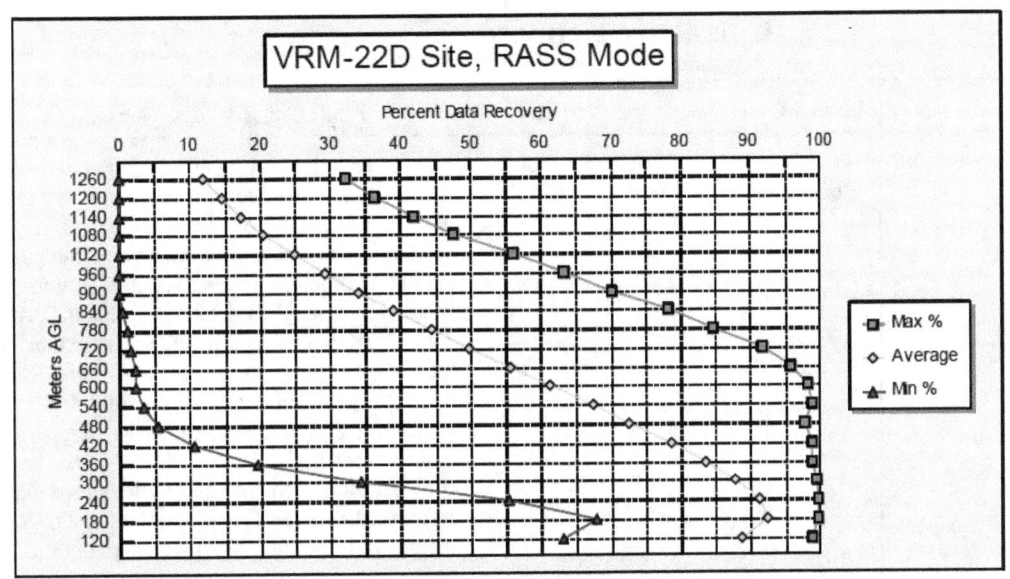

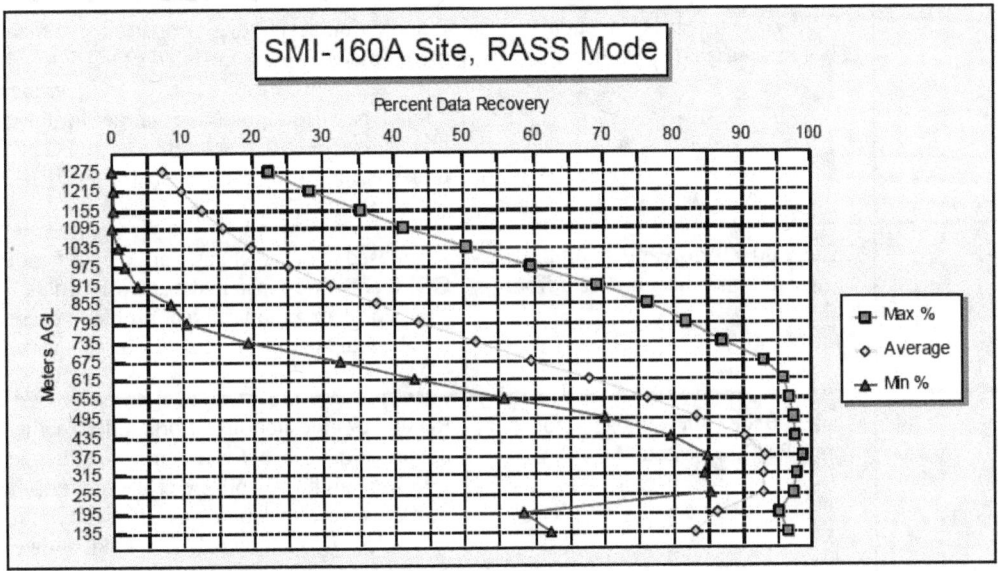

Figure 3-13. Data Recovery Rates for Radar Profiler RASS Mode, September 1999 - August 2000

3.3.5 Problems Encountered and Corrective Action Taken

Table 3-16 lists the problems encountered, and the corrective actions implemented, during the third year of the project.

Table 3-16. Project Year Three Equipment Problems and Corrective Actions

Ref No.	Problem	Project Team Corrective Action
3-1	The radar profilers ceased operation at both sites on 1/1/00.	Remote troubleshooting efforts failed to diagnose the problem. However, it was determined that other (non-MMS) radar profilers using a GPS clock connection to update time stamps on the radar profiler computers were suffering the same problem. It was then determined that the problem was a Y2K problem in the GPS system that caused the computers to stop because they were being told it was the year 1900 rather than 2000. An unscheduled visit to both sites was then performed during the period 1/14/00 to 1/16/00. System configuration changes were implemented that resolved the "wrong year" problem and restored the profilers and GOES data flow to normal operations.
3-2	At VRM22D the surface met data collection ceased on 2/26/00.	Remote troubleshooting efforts failed to diagnose the problem. An unscheduled site visit to VRM22D was performed on 3/24/00, during which a failed power supply in the charger for the data logger was identified and replaced and GOES transmission of surface met data from VRM22D were restored.
3-3	On 2/29/00 a leap year date problem was noted transmitted met data from both sites.	Diagnosed the problem as caused by a fault in the GOES software. Installed a software patch at both sites, correcting the leap year problem, during unscheduled platform visits during the period 3/24/00 - 3/26/00.
3-4	On 4/2/00 the GOES transmissions from VRM22D ceased.	Remote troubleshooting efforts failed to diagnose the problem. Since it was confirmed that the met data were all being collected (just not transmitted), further corrective action was deferred until the next scheduled site visit on 6/14/00. On that date, the problem was found to be due to an interrupt in the Gateway Computer, which was cleared during the visit and GOES transmissions were restored.

Table 3-16. Project Year Three Equipment Problems and Corrective Actions (Cont'd)

Ref No.	Problem	Project Team Corrective Action
3-5	The GOES transmission system was inoperative from 3/30/00 until 4/10/00.	The GOES systems was restored by NESDIS. The project team retrieved the collected data during this period from the computers at the sites during the scheduled visits performed during the period 6/14/00-6/16/00.
3-6	In early April 2000, it was discovered that the data time stamps had again changed to DST even though the configurations were set for them to remain on CST. Note: This is a repeat of the daylight savings time problem that occurred in the late 1999 (see ref item 2-5 in Table 3-12 of this report).	Researched the Microsoft web site and found technical reference information acknowledging this problem and providing a software patch fix. Installed the patch on the computers at both sites during the scheduled site visits performed during the period 6/14/00-6/16/00.
3-7	At VRM22D the temperature/RH sensor failed audit criteria during the 6/14/00 site visit.	Replaced the sensor during the visit.
3-8	At SMI160A the temperature/RH sensor and the SST sensor failed audit criteria during the 6/16/00 site visit.	Replaced both sensors during the visit.
3-9	On 9/8/00 the GOES transmissions from SMI160A ceased.	Remote troubleshooting isolated the problem to a failed GOES DCP. The spare unit was shipped to the platform and installed by platform personnel on 9/27/00, restoring GOES transmissions from SMI160A.

3.3.6 Summary

Tasks completed during the third year of work on this project successfully supported the objective. Sites and equipment were rigorously monitored, problems quickly addressed, and reports submitted on time. All data measurements collected were quality checked on a daily basis and were processed and documented by formal reporting on a monthly basis.

During the third year of the project, the average data capture rate was 86.9%, which did not quite meet the project's 90% or higher goal. As of the end of the third year of the project, the cumulative data capture rate for the project was 90.5%, which met the project's 90% or higher goal.

3.4   Project Year Four Activities (10/01/00 - 01/31/02)

Work accomplished and results achieved during the fourth year of the project, October 1, 2000 through January 31, 2002, are detailed below. During the fourth year of the project the contract was amended by MMS to extend the data collection period from 36 to 40 months.

3.4.1   Management

MMS and contractor participants continued to maintain a highly effective project team working relationship, using e-mail and telephone conferences to coordinate and to resolve potential problems as they arose.

3.4.1.1   Personnel

Table 3-17 shows the key personnel participants in the project during the fourth year. There were no changes of the key personnel participants in the project during the fourth year.

Table 3-17. Project Year Four Key Personnel

Project Function	Person Performing Function	Comments
MMS Contracting Officer (CO)	Wally Adcox	
MMS Contracting Officer's Technical Representative (COTR)	Chester Huang	
Program Manger	Gary Zeigler	Radian (later Vaisala)
Principal Investigator	Tim Dye	STI
Principal Engineer	Bill Burton	Radian (later Vaisala).

3.4.1.2   Communications and Coordination

Authority for all required project team decision actions to ensure timely, efficient, and competent accomplishment of all work under the contract continued to be vested in the Program Manager. Authority for day-to-day decision making continued to be delegated to the Principal Engineer for all equipment-related matters and to the Principal Investigator for all data collection and processing matters.

Routine meetings were conducted by teleconferences as needed.

All formal external communications and coordination by project team members continued to be directed through the Program Manager. Informal communications and coordinating with personnel and agencies outside the project team were encouraged by individual team members as necessary to ensure effective accomplishment of the routine work within the responsibility of the respective team participant. Issues that arose during such informal external contacts were immediately reported through the project management chain to the Program Manager for formal resolution.

3.4.1.3   Record Keeping

The project contract file, including copies of all correspondence with the MMS Contracting Officer, continued to be maintained in the office of the Contract Specialist.

A copy of all documentation related to project accomplishment continued to be maintained in the office of the Program Manager. These documents include all project directives, reports of trips and meetings, record copies of all written deliverables submitted to MMS, and copies of all written correspondence between the Program Manager and the MMS COTR.

Data collection and processing, chain of custody, and other quality assurance records continued to be maintained by the Principal Investigator. These records serve as the basis of monthly and annual reporting, as well as other formal submissions.

Equipment testing, installation, operation, maintenance, and quality assurance records are maintained by the Principal Engineer. The Principal Engineer also continued to maintain a log of all scheduled and unscheduled site visit activities and the results thereof. These records serve as the basis of monthly and annual reporting, as well as other formal submissions, that were initiated by the Principal Engineer, through the Program Manager, to MMS as contract deliverables.

3.4.2   Site and Equipment Preparation Logistics

3.4.2.1   Site Selection

Details on the original site-finding efforts and results are described in Section 3.1.2.1 of this report. To recap, the following two platforms were selected for the study:

1) Vermillion 22D, operated by ERT, as the shallow water site; and

2) South Marsh Island 160A, originally operated by Chevron, and subsequently by Newfield Exploration, as the deep water site.

3.4.2.2   RF Licenses

As described in Section 3.1.2.2 of this report, RF licenses were required (and obtained) for the GOES satellite data up-link and for the wind profiler operating frequency.

- The profiler data were transmitted using a two-minute per hour channel of the NOAA/NESDIS Geostationary Operational Environmental Satellite (GOES) system. Allocation of the channel from NESDIS and permitting from NTIA to transmit to the GOES satellite at 402 MHz were required and received.

- The wind profiler measurements were based on radar pulses centered at 915 MHz. Permission from NTIA to operate the two profilers in the Gulf of Mexico in this band was required and received.

There were no problems with our licenses during the fourth year of the project.

3.4.2.3   Equipment

During the fourth year of the project, there were no changes to the measurement equipment used at the two sites, as previously listed in Table 3-2.

3.4.2.4   Data Processing

The data processing and communications tasks continued to include preparing the data at the sites, transmitting the data back through GOES, receiving the data at the STI Weather Operations Center, analyzing and storing the data, and submitting data reports.

During the fourth year of the project, no procedure or data flow changes were needed or made.

3.4.3   Site Operations and Maintenance

During the fourth year of the project, three scheduled visits and four unscheduled visits were performed, as listed in Table 3-18.

Table 3-18. Project Year Four Site Visits

Visit Date	Site(s) Visited	Visit Type	Visit Tasks Performed
10/23/00 – 10/30/00	VRM22D & SMI160A	Scheduled	Performed periodic equipment audits
			At VRM22D, replaced the surface wind and temp/RH sensors (due to audit results)
1/9/01	SMI160A	Unscheduled	Replaced failed power supply in the Radar Computer (which had also caused the Gateway Computer to interrupt and not send GOES transmissions) and restored system to full operation
1/31/01	VRM22D	Unscheduled	Replaced failed RH sensor, and replaced the SST sensor because calibration was expiring.
3/7/01 – 3/8/01	VRM22D & SMI160A	Unscheduled	At VRM22D, replaced the failed phase shifter in the radar profiler.
			At SMI160A, replaced the suspect RH sensor.
4/25/01 – 4/27/01	SMI160A	Unscheduled	Moved the radar profiler antenna about 30 feet on the SMI160A platform deck to allow room for a drilling rig being installed by the platform owner.
6/4/01 – 6/9/01	VRM22D & SMI160A	Scheduled	Performed periodic equipment audits
			At VRM22D, replaced the temp/RH sensor (due to audit results)
			At SMI160A, replaced the failed phase shifter in the radar profiler. Also replaced the failed UPS unit and the failed GOES DCP. Note: The 40-month data collection period was completed as of 10/2/01. Coordination with the platform owners confirmed agreement that an equipment de-installation visit to each platform should be planned for mid November 2001, to allow necessary intervening time for equipment crates to be moved to the platforms.
11/15/01 – 11/15/01	VRM22D & SMI160A	Scheduled	Performed end-of-project equipment audits
			De-installed equipment

3.4.4   Data Measurements

3.4.4.1   Description

The Gateway computer on each platform continued to collect data from the radar profiler, the surface meteorological instrument datalogger, and the GPS receiver. Once each hour, the latest data continued to be packed into a compressed format and transmitted through the GOES satellite link to a database on the NOAA/NESDIS system in Wallops Island, VA.

Automated procedures in the STI weather operations facility continued to be used to retrieve and unpack the data files. The STI staff continued to review the data daily to ensure that all of the collection systems were operating correctly. At the end of each month, the prior month's data continued to be processed to quality-stamp any suspect and invalid measurements. A monthly data report was then generated. The validated monthly data also continued to be loaded into a database archive.

3.4.4.2   Data Capture Rate

The data capture rate measures the up-time of the integrated data collection and communications systems at each site. It is defined using:

Data Capture Rate = (NumRec/NumPos)*100

where:

NumRec = number of hours of data received at STI during the reporting period
NumPos = number of hours of data possible during the reporting period

The data capture rates for September 2000 through October 2, 2001 from the VRM22D site are shown in Table 3-19, and from the SMI160A site in Table 3-20. The goal of the MMS program is to achieve a capture rate of 90% or higher. The average capture rate for all sensors for the September 2000- October 2001 collection period was 86%. The capture rate for the total program through October 2, 2001 was 89.3%.

Table 3-19.   Data Capture Rates for VRM22D Site, September 2000-October 2, 2001

Date	Upper Air Winds	Upper Air T_v	Surface Met
Sep-00	97.9%	97.9%	97.9%
Oct-00	98.3%	98.3%	90.7%
Nov-00	94.0%	93.9%	86.1%
Dec-00	99.0%	99.0%	99.0%
Jan-01	98.9%	98.9%	98.7%
Feb-01	99.0%	98.8%	99.9%
Mar-01	48.5%	48.3%	95.3%
Apr-01	85.4%	85.0%	86.7%
May-01	81.3%	80.9%	99.6%
Jun-01	93.8%	93.8%	98.6%
Jul-01	99.1%	98.9%	99.1%
Aug-01	92.9%	92.7%	92.9%
Sep 01[1]	97.0%	97.0%	97.0%
Annual Average	91.2%	91.0%	97.0%

[1]Note 1: Through October 2, 2001.

Table 3-20.   Data Capture Rates for SMI160A Site, 2000-October 2, 2001

Date	Upper Air Winds	Upper Air T_v	Surface Met
Sep-00	37.2%	37.2%	37.2%
Oct-00	87.4%	87.4%	96.8%
Nov-00	97.2%	97.1%	78.5%
Dec-00	87.5%	87.4%	97.0%
Jan-01	60.3%	60.2%	60.6%
Feb-01	97.2%	97.0%	97.2%
Mar-01	96.9%	96.9%	96.9%
Apr-01	89.9%	90.1%	91.5%
May-01	76.9%	76.5%	76.9%
Jun-01	67.9%	67.6%	68.3%
Jul-01	72.6%	72.2%	72.6%
Aug-01	91.8%	91.7%	93.0%
Sep 01[1]	88.2%	75.9%	88.2%
Annual Average	80.8%	79.8%	81.1%

[1]Note 1: Through October 2, 2001

3.4.4.3   Data Recovery Rate

The data recovery rate is defined as the percentage of valid data captured by each instrument while the integrated system is operational. It is calculated using:

Data Recovery Rate = (NumVal/NumRec)*100

where:

NumVal = Number of valid hours of data received during the reporting period

NumRec = Number of hours of data received at STI during the reporting period.

The data recovery rate provides a method to evaluate the performance of the instruments.

As of the September 30, 2000 end date of the fourth year of the project, data rates for September 1999 through August 2000 were available (and data for September 2000 were being processed). These figures illustrate data capture rate for each site in a series of graphs that are labeled "Max %", "Average", and "Min %". The graphs are, respectively:

The maximum monthly capture rate over the twelve months in the sample;
The average monthly capture rate over the twelve months in the sample;
The minimum monthly capture rate over the twelve months in the sample.

The horizontal (or x) scale is the percent of data capture and the vertical (or y) scale is the measurement altitude in meters AGL.

3.4.4.3.1 Radar Profiler High-Mode Wind Data

The data recovery rates for the two sites for the high-mode winds are shown in Figure 3-14. The relatively low data recovery rates at low altitudes at the SMI site were attributed to interference from sea clutter. The VRM profiler installation is less sensitive to sea clutter and did not experience similar data losses.

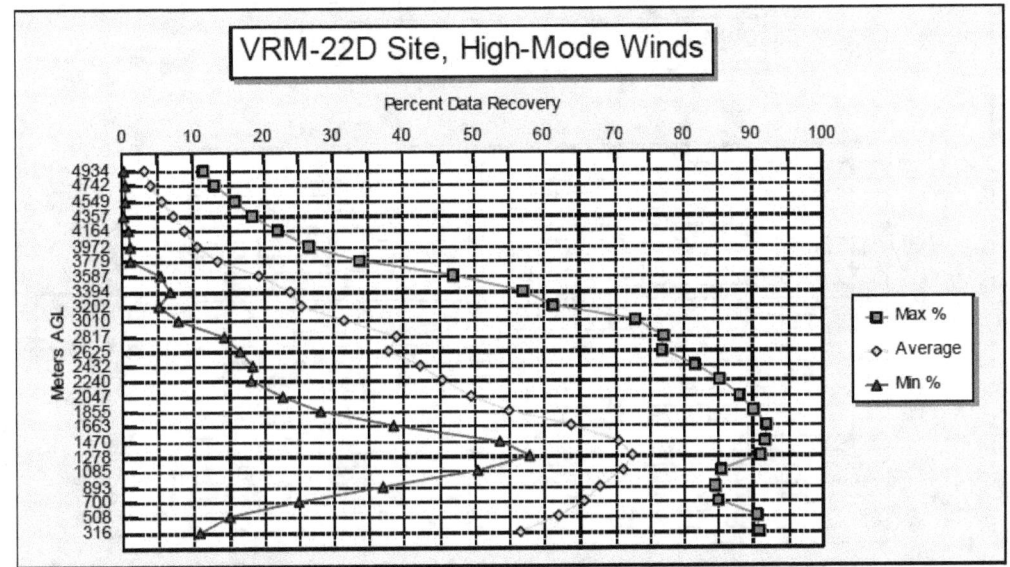

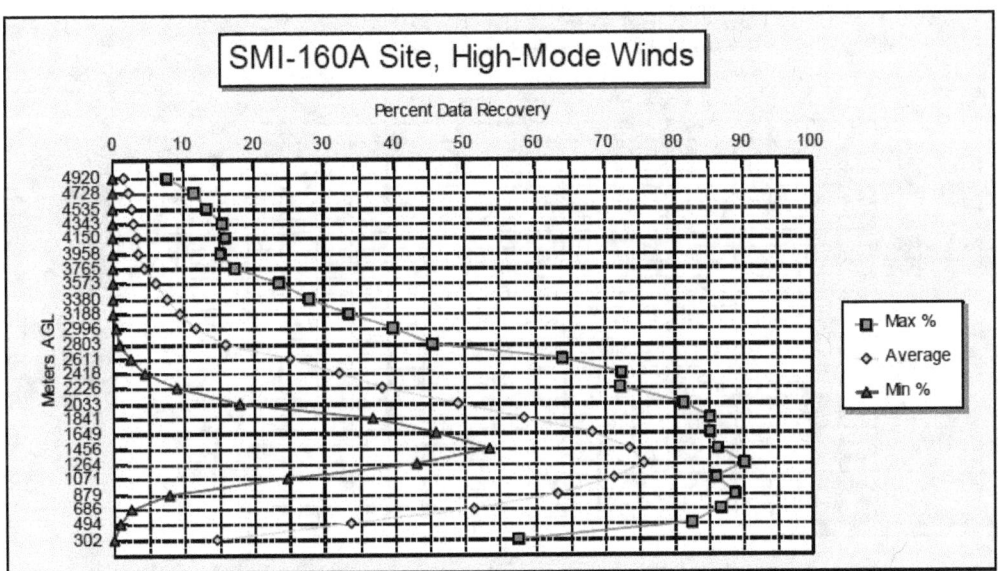

Figure 3-14. **Data Recovery Rates for Radar Profiler High-Mode Winds, September 2000 - October 2, 2001**

3.4.4.3.2   Radar Profiler Low-Mode Wind Data

The data recovery rates for the two sites for the low-mode winds are shown in Figure 3-15. Both sites experienced data recovery losses at the lowest altitudes due primarily to sea clutter interference.

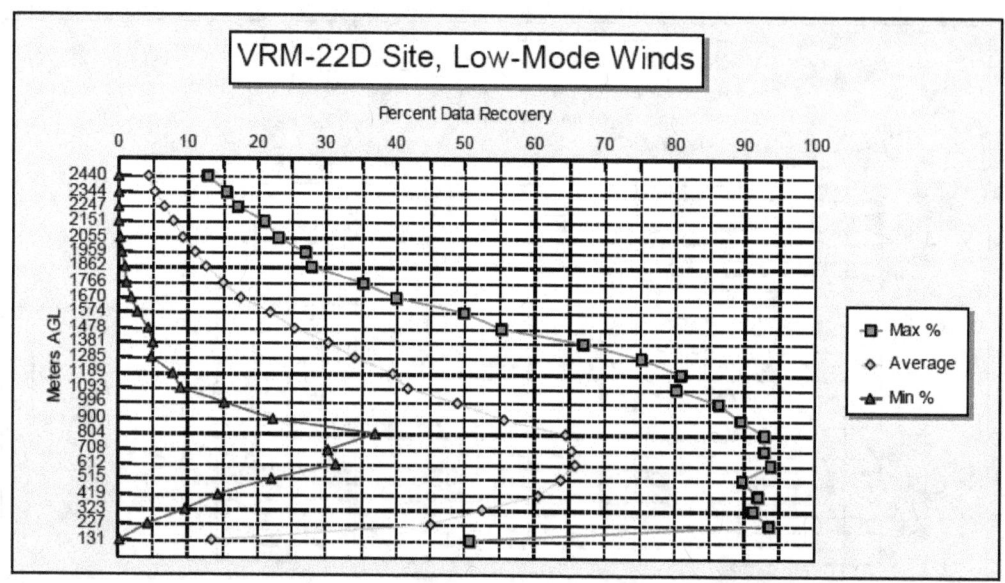

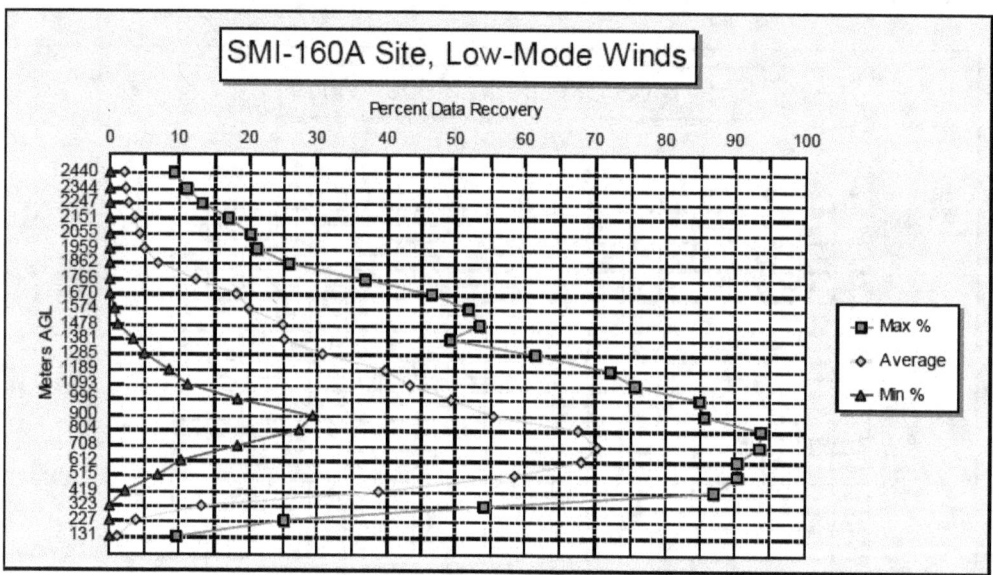

Figure 3-15. Data Recovery Rates for Radar Profiler Low-Mode Winds, September 2000 - October 2, 2001

3.4.4.3.3   RASS Temperature Data

In the RASS mode, virtual temperature profiles are measured by using the scattering of radar pulses from acoustic waves. The data recovery rates for the radar profiler RASS mode are shown in Figure 3-16.

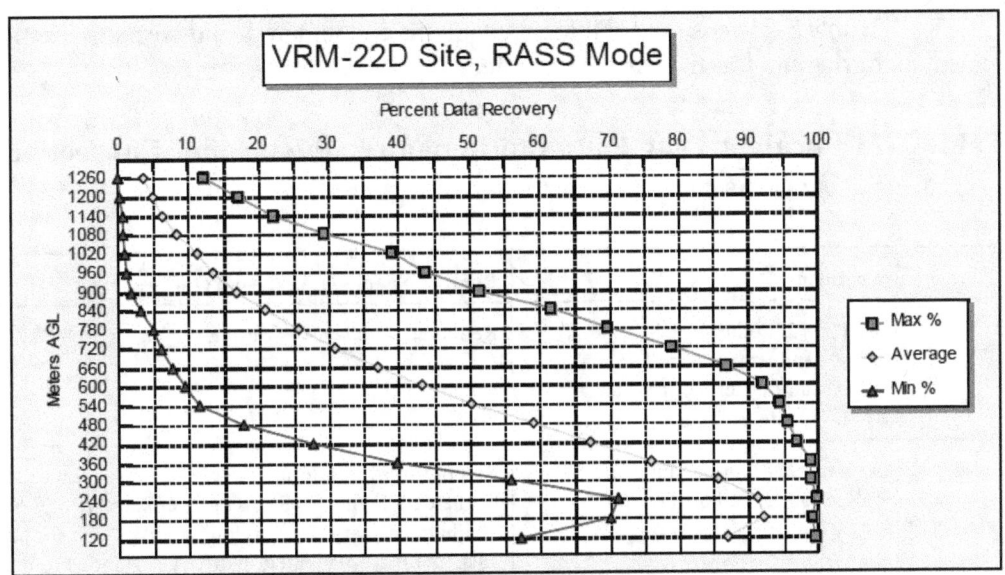

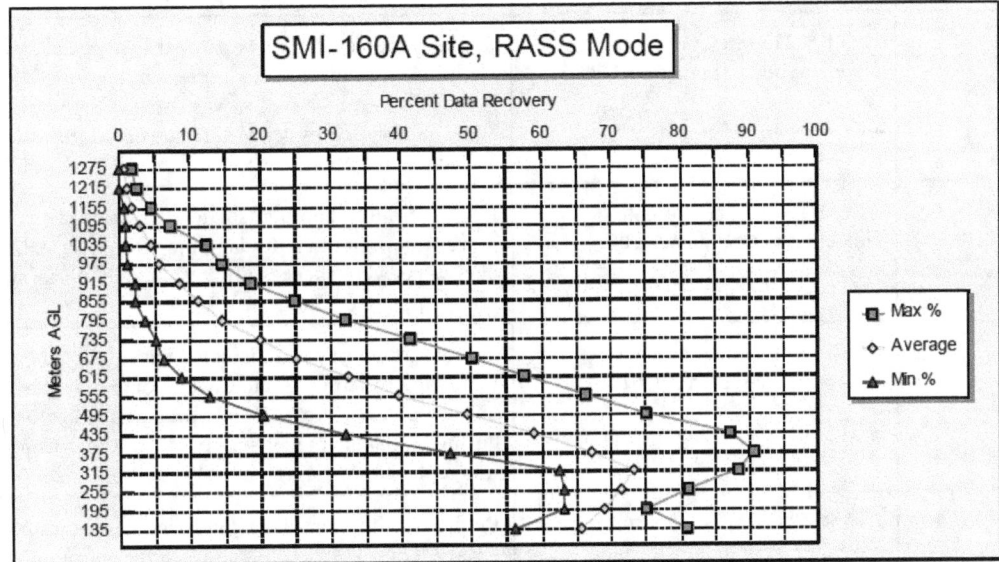

**Figure 3-16. Data Recovery Rates for Radar Profiler RASS Mode,
September 2000 - October 2, 2001**

3.4.5 Problems Encountered and Corrective Action Taken

No problems involving the management of the project were experienced during the fourth year of the project.

Table 3-21 lists the equipment problems encountered, and corrective action implemented, during the fourth year of the project.

Table 3-21. Project Year Four Equipment Problems and Corrective Actions

Ref No.	Problem	Project Team Corrective Action
4 1	At VRM22D the surface wind sensor and temperature/RH sensor failed audit criteria during the 10/23/00 site visit.	Replaced both sensors during the visit.
4 2	At VRM22D surface met data collection ceased on 11/5/00.	Remote troubleshooting isolated the problem to failures of the data logger's 18VAC power supply, 12V battery, and battery charger. A lightning strike was strongly suspected. Replacement parts were shipped to the platform and were installed by VRM22D personnel, restoring surface met data collection on 11/12/00.
4 3	At VRM22D SST sensor data were invalid beginning on 11/8/00.	Remote troubleshooting isolated the suspected cause to a storm having caused water ingestion into the SST sensor. A replacement SST sensor was shipped to the platform and was installed by VRM22D personnel, restoring valid SST data collection.
4 4	At SMI160A upper air data collection ceased on 12/7/00.	Remote troubleshooting isolated the suspected cause to a power interrupt in the Radar Computer. Normal operations were successfully resumed by performing remote power cycling.
4 5	At SMI160A upper air data collection ceased on 1/2/01.	Remote troubleshooting isolated the suspected cause to a failed power supply in the Radar Computer. An unscheduled visit to SMI160A was performed on 1/9/01, during which the power supply in the Radar Computer was replaced, restoring normal operations.
4 6	At VRM22D the RH sensor began providing periodically unstable readings in December 2000 and January 2001.	Replaced with spare during unscheduled visit to VRM22D on 1/25/01. As a target of opportunity, the SST sensor at VRM22D was also replaced (with a freshly calibrated SST sensor) during this visit.

Table 3-21. Project Year Four Equipment Problems and Corrective Actions (Cont'd)

Ref No.	Problem	Project Team Corrective Action
4-7	On 2/28/01, after closely monitoring for some time the VRM22D upper air wind directions being reported by the radar profiler at that site, the STI data processing center alerted project field team participants of a possible problem with that radar profiler.	Data symptoms provided by STI and remote troubleshooting of the site's computer data system suggested a diagnosis of a failed phase shifter in the radar profiler. An unscheduled visit to VRM22D was performed on 3/7/01, during which the failed phase shifter was replaced. STI subsequently reported that this action corrected the wind data quality problem previously observed.
4-8	At SMI160A the RH sensor began providing periodically unstable readings in February 2001.	Replaced with spare during unscheduled visit to SMI160A on 3/8/01.
4-9	In early April 2001, Newfield Exploration notified the project team that the radar profiler antenna on their SMI160A platform would need to be moved about 30 feet before the end April 2001.	Performed an unscheduled visit to SMI160A during the period 4/25/01 – 4/27/01 and moved the radar profiler antenna as required by Newfield.

Note: This action complied with the Newfield requirement. However, the team could do nothing to mitigate the data quality impact that the addition of the drilling rig to the SMI160A platform had on the MMS project. Since the MMS data collection period was nearing completion, it was not economical to relocate the equipment to another platform at that point in the project and it was left in place at SMI160A to gather whatever useful data was possible during the Newfield drilling operations. Primary impacts were that the RASS had to be shut off to preclude bothering the drilling workers on the platform around the clock, and the upper air winds and surface met data both experienced reduced quality due to the physical obstruction posed by the presence of the drilling rig in close proximity to the meteorological measurement equipment. |
| 4-10 | In May 2001 the STI data processing center alerted project field team participants of a possible problem with the SMI160A wind direction measurements. | Data symptoms provided by STI and remote troubleshooting of the site's computer data system suggested the diagnosis of a failed phase shifter in the site's radar profiler. That phase shifter was replaced during the scheduled site visit to SMI160A on 6/9/01. This action restored the radar profiler to normal operation, although interference from the drilling rig continued to cause SMI160A upper air data to be of little value. |
| 4-11 | At the end of May 2001 the GOES transmissions from SMI160A ceased. | Replaced the failed GOES DCP unit at SMI160A during a scheduled visit to the site on 6/9/01. |

Table 3-21. Project Year Four Site/Equipment Problems and Corrective Actions (Cont'd)

Ref No.	Problem	Project Team Corrective Action
4-12	At VRM22D the temperature/RH sensor failed audit criteria during the 6/4/01 site visit.	Replaced the sensor during the visit.
4-13	At VRM22D the RH sensor began providing periodically unstable readings in July 2001.	Replacement was scheduled for the opportune site visit, but no further site visits occurred prior to the end of the data collection period.

3.4.6   Summary

Tasks completed during the fourth year of work on this project successfully supported the objective. Sites and equipment were rigorously monitored, problems quickly addressed, and reports submitted on time. All data measurements collected were quality checked on a daily basis and were processed and documented by formal reporting on a monthly basis.

During the fourth year of the project, the average daily capture rate was 86.0%, which did not quite meet the project's 90% or higher goal. As of the end of the fourth year of the project, the cumulative data capture rate for the project was 89.3% which was slightly below the project's 90% or greater goal.

4.0 DATA COLLECTION RESULTS

As planned, data were collected for a continuous 40-month period at two Gulf of Mexico platform sites, VRM22D and SMI160A, beginning on June 3, 1998 and concluding on October 2, 2001. Upper air data were collected using a 915 MHz pulsed-Doppler radar profiler, with RASS, installed at each site, and included wind direction, wind speed, and virtual temperature. Surface (platform level) data were collected using a suite of standard in-situ meteorological sensors installed at each site, and included wind direction, wind speed, temperature, relative humidity, and pressure. Sea surface temperature data were also collected using a remote-sensing infrared sensor that was installed at platform level at each site and pointed downward to make measurements of water surface temperature. All measurement equipment used was owned by MMS, was installed by project team personnel prior to the data collection period, and was removed by project team personnel following the data collection period.

All data measurements were made and transmitted from each site each hour throughout the data collection period. Site GPS equipment kept data time stamps synchronized and current. Site communications equipment was pre-programmed to transmit collected hourly data from each site, at assigned channel times, via the GOES satellite communications link. All successfully-transmitted data were received and immediately quality checked at the project teams's data center at Sonoma Technology, Inc. in Petaluma, California. Data were also made available in real time to NOAA's Forecast Systems Laboratory in Boulder, Colorado.

4.1 Site Equipment Maintenance and Audit Performance

Project field team personnel diagnosed and corrected equipment problems remotely when possible, and by performing unscheduled site visits as necessary. Visits to both sites were also performed on a scheduled basis to perform equipment preventive maintenance and periodic audits.

4.1.1 Data Collection Remote Maintenance Results

Project data center personnel alerted project field site operations and maintenance personnel when data non-receipt or data quality deficiencies made site equipment checks necessary. These checks were first attempted by remote telephone connection to the site's Gateway Computer, with corrective action also implemented remotely if possible either by remote adjustments to the computer or by getting help from platform personnel to perform simple equipment checks or adjustments.

Attempts to diagnose and correct site data measurement and communications equipment problems remotely were necessary and were performed during almost every month of the data collection period. In the great majority of cases, the remote maintenance attempt was in response to the project data center reporting either no GOES data files being received or GOES data files being received empty of data. These frequent interrupts in data flow that occurred throughout the project were normally due to an interrupt occurring in the controlling GOES, GPS, Radar Computer, or Gateway Computer hardware or software at the impacted site. Remote troubleshooting was normally possible very quickly by dial-in telephone modem connection to the Gateway Computer. Where diagnosis or resets could not be accomplished remotely, attempts were then made to contact platform personnel by telephone and solicit there help in performing needed checks and resets.

Data collection results were benefited by the quick-response remote maintenance actions implemented throughout the project. However, in spite of these efforts, data recovery rates were often negatively impacted by two factors. First, significant delays in connecting to site modems were regularly experienced due to poor quality telephone lines servicing the platforms. Second, significant delays in obtaining platform personnel assistance to perform even very simple and quick diagnostic and corrective actions were increasingly experienced throughout the project. This was always, and understandably, because platform personnel had to complete their primary duties before they could provide the project team the requested assistance. During the early stages of the project, however, the delay (and associated data loss time period) was normally only a few hours, whereas during the latter stages of the project, it was frequently several days. At SMI160A, in particular, it was evident that platform personnel were fully occupied with active drilling operations during the latter stage of the data collection period.

4.1.2   Data Collection On-Site Maintenance Results

When corrective maintenance could not be performed remotely, an unscheduled site visit was planned and performed as quickly as possible. Time delays in performing unscheduled site visits, and therefore data loss impacts, were most frequently dictated by the availability of helicopter transportation to the platforms. Commercial helicopter charter was normally readily available (except during storm evacuations), but was only used in the most urgent situations because of the high cost. Platform-owner provided helicopter transportation was used for most visits. This required project team members to travel on a space-available basis, and resultant delays in reaching platform sites to complete repairs and restore data collection operations were experienced.

Site corrective maintenance visits were performed as listed in Table 4-1.

Table 4-1. Site Corrective Maintenance Visits, June 3, 1998 - October 2, 2001

Site Visit Date	Site Visited	Corrective Maintenance Tasks Performed
9/14/98	VRM22D	Restored GOES transmissions by clearing a Gateway Computer interrupt.
10/9/98	VRM22D	Replaced failed SST sensor.
10/10/98	SMI160A	Replaced GOES DCP unit (because platform had broken the power switch on the original DCP when they attempted to power site equipment back up after Hurricane Georges evacuation).
12/17/98	VRM22D	Replaced failed SST sensor. Also replaced RH sensor as precaution because it appeared to be becoming unstable.
8/6/99	VRM22D	Repaired radar profiler components damaged by lightning strike. Restored GOES transmission of upper air data. Could not make lightning damage repairs needed to restore GOES transmission of surface met data, but confirmed surface data being collected.
9/29/99	VRM22D	Made remaining lightning strike damage repairs and restored GOES transmission of surface met data. Also added surge protection to help better protect equipment against future lightning strikes. Also replace short-haul modem with direct RS-232 connection to improve met data transfer.
9/30/99	SMI160A	Restored GOES transmissions by clearing a Gateway Computer interrupt. Removed a failed UPS and made arrangements for platform personnel to ship it to Vaisala for repair. Also added surge protection to help better protect equipment against future lightning strikes.
1/14/00	VRM22D	Corrected a GPS Y2K problem that had caused the radar profiler to cease operations on 1/1/00 because it was being told the year was 1900.
1/16/00	SMI160A	Corrected a GPS Y2K problem that had caused the radar profiler to cease operations on 1/1/00 because it was being told the year was 1900.
3/24/00	VRM22D	Replaced failed power supply in the charger for the data logger and restored GOES transmissions of surface met data. Replaced the radar profiler=s final amplifier unit as a precaution because of potential performance degradation. Installed a software patch to help prevent future leap year problems.
3/26/00	SMI160A	Installed a software patch to help prevent future leap year problems.
6/14/00	VRM22D	Restored GOES transmissions by clearing a Gateway Computer interrupt. Installed a Windows 95 patch to help keep time stamps at CST all year.
6/16/00	SMI160A	Installed repaired UPS unit (previously removed during 9/30/99 visit. Installed a Windows 95 patch to help keep time stamps at CST all year.

Table 4-1. Site Corrective Maintenance Visits,
June 3, 1998 - October 2, 2001 (Cont'd)

Site Visit Date	Site Visited	Corrective Maintenance Tasks Performed
1/9/01	SMI160A	Replaced failed power supply in the Radar Computer and restored equipment operation and GOES data transmissions.
1/31/01	VRM22D	Replaced failed RH sensor. Replaced the SST sensor because its calibration was expiring.
3/7/01	VRM22D	Replaced failed radar profiler phase shifter RF relays.
3/8/01	SMI160A	Replaced the RH sensor because its data were becoming unstable.
4/27/01	SMI160A	Moved the radar profiler antenna about 30 feet on the platform deck to make room for a drilling rig being installed by the platform owner.
6/9/01	SMI160A	Replaced failed radar profiler phase shifter RF relays. Also replaced failed UPS and GOES DCP units

4.1.3   Data Collection Equipment Audit Results

Audits of site equipment significantly enhanced data collection results by detecting and correcting equipment problems in a timely manner. Audits were planned on approximately a six month basis. Actual audit frequency was adjusted to merge audits with unscheduled corrective maintenance visits where reasonable and most cost effective. A total of nine audits were performed during the 40-month data collection period, including the readiness audit prior to the start of data collection and the final audit following the completion of data collection. All audits included both upper air and surface measurement equipment at both sites. A list of audits performed and equipment components that failed audit criteria and were replaced during the audit visit is shown in Table 4-2. The sensors that most frequently failed audit criteria and that required replacement were the relative humidity and sea surface temperature sensors.

Table 4-2. Site Equipment Audit Visits

Month Audit Performed	Sites Audited	Audit Results
March 1998 (Readiness Audit Before Start of Data Collection Period)	VRM22D	All Sensors Passed
	SMI160A	All Sensors Passed
September 1998	VRM22D	All Sensors Passed
	SMI160A	All Sensors Passed
April 1999	VRM22D	All Sensors Passed
	SMI160A	Replaced Corroded SST Sensor
September 1999	VRM22D	Replaced Temp/RH Sensor
	SMI160A	All Sensors Passed
January 2000	VRM22D	All Sensors Passed
	SMI160A	All Sensors Passed
June 2000	VRM22DI	Replaced Temp/RH Sensor
	SMI160A	Replaced Temp/RH & SST Sensors
October 2000	VRM22D	Replaced Temp/RH & Wind Sensors
	SMI160A	All Sensors Passed
June 2001	VRM22D	Replaced Temp/RH Sensor
	SMI160A	Replaced Radar Profiler Phase Shifter RF Relays
November 2001 (Final Audit After End of Data Collection Period)	VRM22D	Temp/RH Sensor Failed Audit
	SMI160A	All Sensors Passed

4.2   Data Capture Results

One of the goals of the project was to achieve an overall data capture rate of 90% or higher. The actual data capture rate achieved during the 40-month data collection period was 89.3%, slightly below the goal. Except for factors beyond the project team's control that impacted data collection results, the data capture rate achieved during the 40-month data collection period would have been well above the 90% goal. Example impacts on data rates that could not be controlled included equipment power shutdowns for tropical storm and hurricane evacuations, equipment damage due to lightning strikes, and equipment operating restrictions caused by the addition of a drilling rig to one of the platform sites.

Average data capture rate results for the 40-month data collection period are listed by data types, sites, and data months in Table 4-3, Table 4-4, and Table 4-5. Months with poorest average data capture rates and cause factors are listed in Table 4-6.

Table 4-3. VRM22D Monthly Data Capture Rates, June 3, 1998 – October 2, 2001

Month /Year	Upper Air Wind Average Data Capture Rate for the Month	Upper Air Temperature Average Data Capture Rate for the Month	Surface Met Data Average Data Capture Rate for the Month	All Data Types Average Data Capture Rate for the Month	All Data Types Running Average Data Capture Rate for all Months to Date in Project
06/98	99.3%	99.3%	99.3%	99.3%	99.3%
07/98	93.8%	93.8%	93.8%	93.8%	96.6%
08/98	97.0%	97.0%	97.0%	97.0%	96.7%
09/98	80.7%	81.0%	100.0%	87.2%	94.3%
10/98	95.2%	95.3%	95.3%	95.3%	94.5%
11/98	96.8%	96.7%	96.9%	96.8%	94.9%
12/98.	97.3%	97.3%	97.3%	97.3%	95.2%
01/99	94.2%	94.2%	94.2%	94.2%	95.1%
02/99	97.6%	97.6%	97.6%	97.6%	95.4%
03/99	95.4%	95.4%	95.8%	95.5%	95.4%
04/99	74.4%	74.4%	71.9%	73.6%	93.4%
05/99	97.9%	97.9%	98.7%	98.2%	93.8%
06/99	72.8%	72.6%	72.4%	72.6%	92.2%
07/99	98.8%	91.8%	98.8%	96.5%	92.5%
08/99	87.0%	78.4%	8.7%	58.0%	90.2%

Table 4-3. VRM22D Monthly Data Capture Rates, June 3, 1998 – October 2, 2001 (Cont'd)

Month /Year	Upper Air Wind Average Data Capture Rate for the Month	Upper Air Temperature Average Data Capture Rate for the Month	Surface Met Data Average Data Capture Rate for the Month	All Data Types Average Data Capture Rate for the Month	All Data Types Running Average Data Capture Rate for all Months to Date in Project
09/99	96.7%	96.7%	1.4%	64.9%	88.6%
10/99	95.8%	95.7%	96.8%	96.1%	89.1%
11/99	96.5%	96.5%	96.4%	96.5%	89.5%
12/99	90.5%	90.3%	90.6%	90.5%	89.5%
01/00	49.9%	49.7%	94.5%	64.7%	88.3%
02/00	93.7%	93.7%	84.2%	90.5%	88.4%
03/00	60.2%	60.1%	23.7%	48.0%	86.6%
04/00	99.9%	99.9%	99.9%	99.9%	87.1%
05/00	98.7%	98.5%	100.0%	99.1%	87.7%
06/00	76.1%	59.0%	96.4%	77.2%	87.2%
07/00	98.0%	98.0%	98.0%	98.0%	87.7%
08/00	99.9%	99.9%	99.9%	99.9%	88.1%
09/00	97.9%	97.9%	97.9%	97.9%	88.5%
10/00	98.3%	98.3%	90.7%	95.8%	88.7%
11/00	94.0%	93.9%	86.1%	91.3%	88.8%
12/00	99.0%	99.0%	99.0%	99.0%	89.1%
01/01	98.9%	98.9%	98.7%	98.8%	89.4%
02/01	99.0%	98.8%	99.9%	99.2%	89.7%
03/01	48.5%	48.3%	95.3%	64.0%	89.0%
04/01	85.4%	85.0%	86.7%	85.7%	88.9%
05/01	81.3%	80.9%	99.6%	87.3%	88.8%

Table 4-3. VRM22D Monthly Data Capture Rates,
June 3, 1998 – October 2, 2001 (Cont'd)

Month/ Year	Upper Air Wind Average Data Capture Rate for the Month	Upper Air Temperature Average Data Capture Rate for the Month	Surface Met Data Average Data Capture Rate for the Month	All Data Types Average Data Capture Rate for the Month	All Data Types Running Average Data Capture Rate for all Months to Date in Project
06/01	93.8%	93.8%	98.6%	95.4%	89.0%
07/01	99.1%	98.9%	99.1%	99.0%	89.3%
08/01	92.9%	92.7%	92.9%	92.8%	89.4%
09/01	97.0%	97.0%	97.0%	97.0%	89.6%
All 40 Months	90.5%	89.6%	88.5%	89.6%	89.6%

Table 4-4. SMI160A Monthly Data Capture Rates,
June 3, 1998 – October 2, 2001

Month /Year	Upper Air Wind Average Data Capture Rate for the Month	Upper Air Temperature Average Data Capture Rate for the Month	Surface Met Data Average Data Capture Rate for the Month	All Data Types Average Data Capture Rate for the Month	All Data Types Running Average Data Capture Rate for all Months to Date in Project
06/98	98.2%	98.2%	98.2%	98.2%	98.2%
07/98	97.4%	96.2%	97.5%	97.0%	97.6%
08/98	99.7%	99.7%	99.6%	99.7%	98.3%
09/98	85.3%	85.5%	100.0%	90.3%	96.3%
10/98	90.7%	91.0%	87.6%	89.8%	95.0%
11/98	98.9%	98.8%	99.0%	98.9%	95.6%

Table 4-4. SMI160A Monthly Data Capture Rates, June 3, 1998 – October 2, 2001 (Cont'd)

Month /Year	Upper Air Wind Average Data Capture Rate for the Month	Upper Air Temperature Average Data Capture Rate for the Month	Surface Met Data Average Data Capture Rate for the Month	All Data Types Average Data Capture Rate for the Month	All Data Types Running Average Data Capture Rate for all Months to Date in Project
12/98	87.5%	87.4%	94.8%	89.9%	94.8%
01/99	99.5%	99.5%	99.5%	99.5%	95.4%
02/99	96.1%	96.1%	96.1%	96.1%	95.5%
03/99	97.7%	97.7%	98.1%	97.8%	95.7%
04/99	98.9%	99.0%	99.3%	99.1%	96.0%
05/99	98.5%	98.5%	99.3%	98.8%	96.3%
06/99	98.1%	98.1%	98.1%	98.1%	96.4%
07/99	97.9%	97.9%	97.9%	97.9%	96.5%
08/99	99.3%	99.5%	99.5%	99.4%	96.7%
09/99	79.4%	79.4%	76.0%	78.3%	95.6%
10/99	69.5%	69.4%	83.7%	74.2%	94.3%
11/99	99.2%	99.2%	99.2%	99.2%	94.6%
12/99	94.2%	94.1%	97.7%	95.3%	94.6%
01/00	38.2%	40.5%	62.9%	47.2%	92.2%
02/00	96.8%	96.8%	97.0%	96.9%	92.5%
03/00	98.5%	98.5%	98.5%	98.5%	92.7%
04/00	95.0%	94.9%	95.0%	95.0%	92.8%
05/00	96.1%	96.2%	97.3%	96.5%	93.0%
06/00	97.1%	96.8%	96.4%	96.8%	93.1%
07/00	92.7%	92.6%	92.7%	92.7%	93.1%

Table 4-4. SMI160A Monthly Data Capture Rates,
June 3, 1998 - October 2, 2001 (Cont'd)

Month/Year	Upper Air Wind Average Data Capture Rate for the Month	Upper Air Temperature Average Data Capture Rate for the Month	Surface Met Data Average Data Capture Rate for the Month	All Data Types Average Data Capture Rate for the Month	All Data Types Running Average Data Capture Rate for all Months to Date in Project
08/00	90.5%	90.5%	90.5%	90.5%	93.0%
09/00	37.2%	37.2%	37.2%	37.2%	91.0%
10/00	87.4%	87.4%	96.8%	90.5%	91.0%
11/00	97.2%	97.1%	78.5%	90.9%	91.0%
12/00	87.5%	87.4%	97.0%	90.6%	91.0%
01/01	60.3%	60.2%	60.6%	60.4%	90.0%
02/01	97.2%	97.0%	97.2%	97.1%	90.3%
03/01	96.9%	96.9%	96.9%	96.9%	90.4%
04/01	89.9%	90.1%	91.5%	90.5%	90.4%
05/01	76.9%	76.5%	76.9%	76.8%	90.1%
06/01	67.9%	67.6%	68.3%	67.9%	89.5%
07/01	72.6%	72.2%	72.6%	72.5%	89.0%
08/01	91.8%	91.7%	93.0%	92.2%	89.1%
09/01	88.2%	75.9%	88.2%	84.1%	89.0%
All 40 Months	88.5%	88.2%	90.2%	89.0%	89.0%

Table 4-5. Combined VRM22D & SMI160A Monthly Data Capture Rates, June 3, 1998 - October 2, 2001

Month /Year	Upper Air Wind Average Data Capture Rate for the Month	Upper Air Temperature Average Data Capture Rate for the Month	Surface Met Data Average Data Capture Rate for the Month	All Data Types Average Data Capture Rate for the Month	All Data Types Running Average Data Capture Rate for all Months to Date in Project
06/98	98.8%	98.8%	98.8	98.8%	98.8%
07/98	95.6%	95.0%	95.7	95.4%	97.1%
08/98	98.4%	98.4%	98.3	98.4%	97.5%
09/98	83.0%	83.3%	100.0	88.8%	95.4%
10/98	93.0%	93.2%	91.5	92.6%	94.8%
11/98	97.8%	97.8%	98.0	97.9%	95.3%
12/98.	92.4%	92.4%	96.1	93.6%	95.1%
01/99	94.9%	96.9%	96.9%	96.2%	95.2%
02/99	96.8%	96.9%	96.9%	96.9%	95.4%
03/99	96.6%	96.6%	95.5%	96.2%	95.5%
04/99	86.7%	86.7%	85.6%	86.3%	94.6%
05/99	98.2%	98.2%	99.0%	98.5%	95.0%
06/99	85.5%	85.4%	85.3%	85.4%	94.2%
07/99	98.4%	94.9%	98.4%	97.2%	94.4%
08/99	93.2%	89.0%	54.1%	78.8%	93.4%
09/99	88.1%	88.1%	38.7%	71.6%	92.0%
10/99	82.7%	82.6%	90.3%	85.2%	91.6%
11/99	97.9%	97.9%	97.8%	97.9%	92.0%
12/99	92.4%	92.2%	94.2%	92.3%	92.0%
01/00	44.1%	45.1%	78.7%	56.0%	90.2%

Table 4-5. Combined VRM22D & SMI160A Monthly Data Capture Rates, June 3, 1998 - October 2, 2001 (Cont'd)

Month/ Year	Upper Air Wind Average Data Capture Rate for the Month	Upper Air Temperature Average Data Capture Rate for the Month	Surface Met Data Average Data Capture Rate for the Month	All Data Types Average Data Capture Rate for the Month	All Data Types Running Average Data Capture Rate for all Months to Date in Project
02/00	95.3%	95.3%	90.6%	93.7%	90.4%
03/00	79.4%	79.3%	61.1%	73.3%	89.6%
04/00	97.5%	97.4%	97.5%	97.5%	89.9%
05/00	97.4%	97.4%	98.7%	97.8%	90.3%
06/00	86.6%	77.9%	96.4%	87.0%	90.1%
07/00	95.4%	95.3%	95.4%	95.4%	90.3%
08/00	95.2%	95.2%	95.2%	95.2%	90.5%
09/00	67.6%	67.6%	67.6%	67.6%	89.7%
10/00	92.9%	92.9%	93.8%	93.2%	89.8%
11/00	95.6%	95.5%	82.3%	91.1%	89.9%
12/00	93.3%	93.2%	98.0%	94.8%	90.0%
01/01	79.6%	79.6%	80.2%	79.8%	89.7%
02/01	98.1%	97.9%	98.6%	98.2%	90.0%
03/01	72.7%	72.6%	96.1%	80.5%	89.7%
04/01	87.7%	87.5%	89.1%	88.1%	89.6%
05/01	79.1%	78.7%	88.3%	82.0%	89.4%
06/01	80.9%	80.7%	83.5%	81.7%	89.2%
07/01	85.9%	85.6%	85.9%	85.8%	89.1%
08/01	92.4%	92.2%	93.0%	92.5%	89.2%
09/01	92.6%	86.5%	92.6%	90.6%	89.3%
All 40 Months	89.5%	88.9%	89.4%	89.3%	89.3%

Table 4-6. Poor Data Capture Rate Months and Cause Factors

Month/Year	Poor Data Capture Rate	Cause Factors
04/99	VRM22D All data 72-74%	GOES transmitter failure and computer time-keeping failure (due to platform power instability).
06/99	VRM22D All data ~72%	GOES software interrupt, complicated by phone outage at platform that delayed contact with platform personnel to correct the GOES problem.
08/99	VRM22D Surface met data 8.7%	Lightning strike damage.
09/99	VRM22D Surface met data 1.4%	Lightning strike damage (continuation of outage that began in early August and was repaired in late September).
01/00	VRM22D Upper air data ~50%	Radar Profiler outage due to GPS Y2K problem (which caused the radar profiler computers to stop because they were given the year 1900 instead of 2000 by the GPS). Required extensive time to find and fix the problem).
03/00	VRM22D Surface met data ~24%	Power supply failure in the charger for the data logger.
03/00	VRM22D Upper air data ~60%	Radar Computer software interrupts.
06/00	VRM22D Upper air data 59-76%	Gateway Computer software interrupts.
03/01	VRM22D Upper air data ~48%	Gateway Computer software interrupts (complicated by delays in platform personnel availability to help resolve).
09/00	SMI160A All data ~79%	Gateway Computer interrupt and failed UPS unit (due to platform power problems).
10/99	SMI160A Upper air data ~69%	Radar Computer and Software Computer software interrupts.
01/00	SMI160A Upper air data ~39%	Radar profiler outage due to GPS Y2K problem (which caused the radar profiler computers to stop because they were given the year 1900 instead of 2000 by the GPS). Required extensive time to find and fix the problem.
01/00	SMI160A Surface met data ~63%	GOES software interrupts.
09/00	SMI160A All data ~37%	GOES transmitter failure.

Table 4-6. Poor Data Capture Rate Months and Cause Factors (Cont'd)

Month/Year	Poor Data Capture Rate	Cause Factors
11/00	SMI160A Surface met data ~79%	Data logger power supply, battery and charger failure (suspected lightning strike).
01/01	SMI160A All data ~60%	Radar Computer power supply failure (which also caused the Gateway Computer to stop).
05/01	SMI160A All data ~76%	Platform power fluctuations and shutdowns (due to drilling operations in progress).
06/01	SMI160A All data ~68%	Platform power fluctuations and shutdowns (due to drilling operations in progress) and GOES transmitter failure.
07/01	SMI160A All data ~72%	Gateway and Radar Computer software interrupts (complicated by delays in platform personnel availability to help resolve).
09/01	SMI160A Upper air temp~76%	Gateway and Radar Computer software interrupts (complicated by delays in platform personnel availability to help resolve).

4.3   Data Recovery Results

Data recovery rates achieved for the 40-month data collection period are shown in Figure 4-1, Figure 4-2, and Figure 4-3 for upper air data and in Table 4-7 for the surface meteorological data. These recovery rates are about as expected for similar projects using radar profilers and surface sensors of the type employed for this project. Recovery rates for radar profilers are heavily dependent upon the height to which upper air winds and temperatures can be measured based upon atmospheric conditions. Also, as used on platform sites in this project, the lowest heights at which upper air winds and temperatures can be measured by a radar profiler is limited by interference from the platform structure itself and by interference from the Doppler shift of wave movements in the vicinity of the platform site (within the sidelobe viewing distance of the radar).

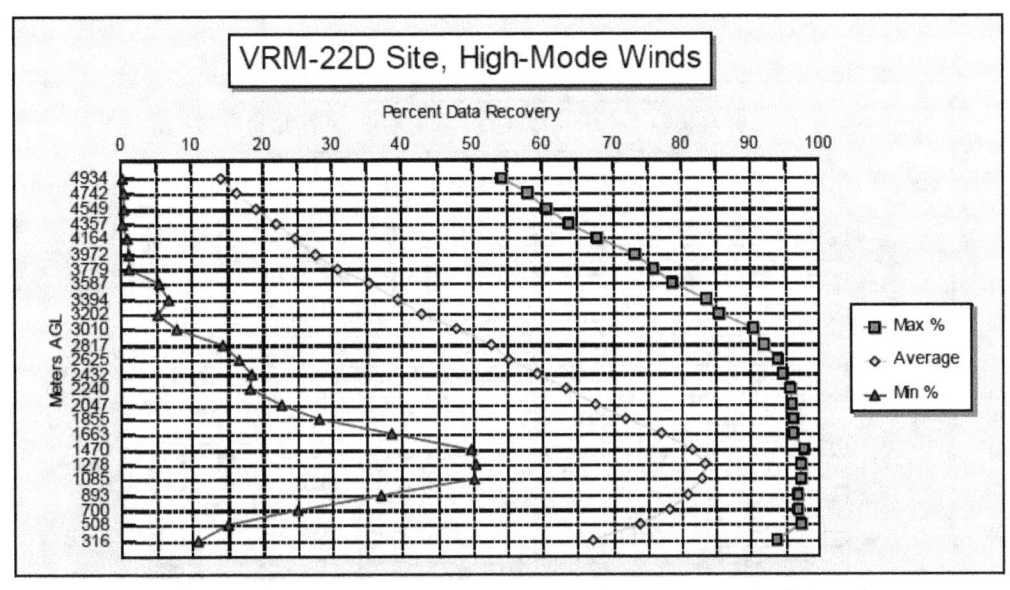

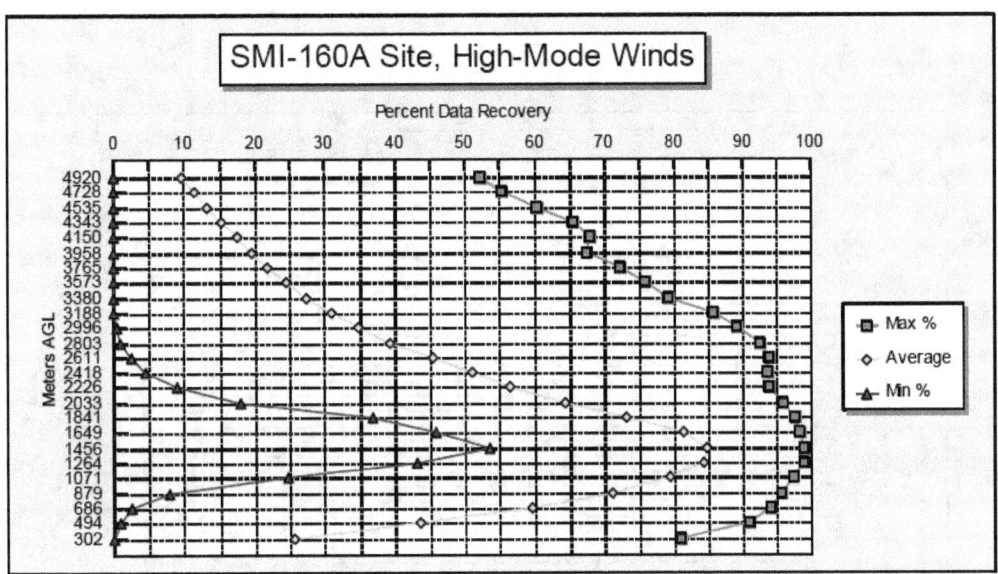

Figure 4-1. **Data Recovery Rates for Radar Profiler High-Mode Winds, June 3, 1998 - October 2, 2001**

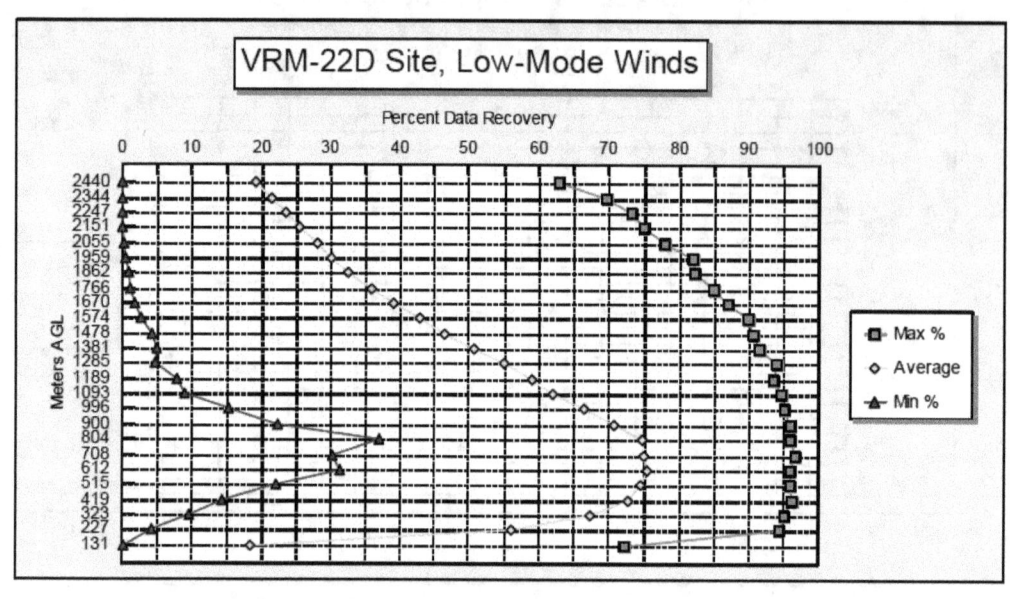

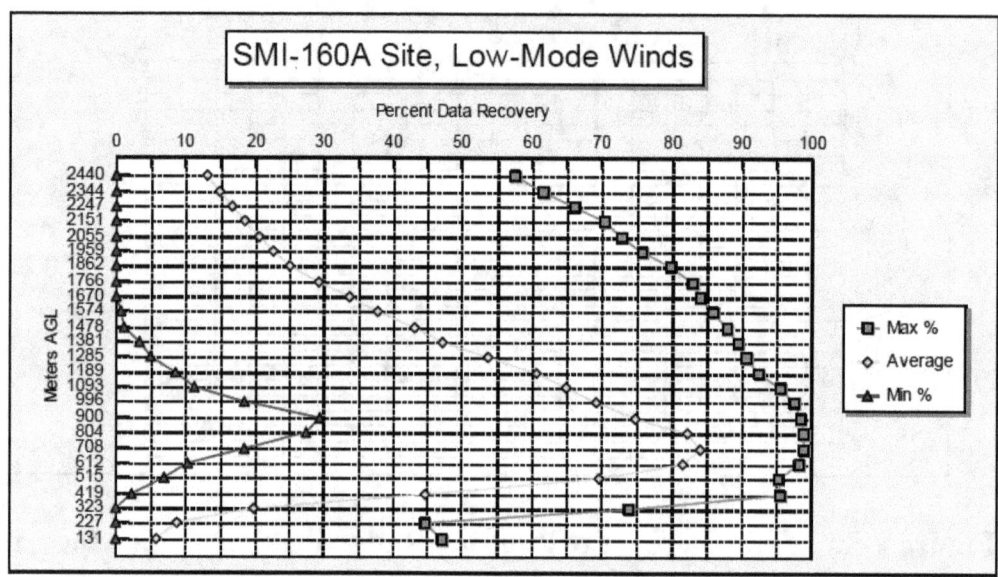

Figure 4-2. Data Recovery Rates for Radar Profiler Low-Mode Winds, June 3, 1998 - October 2, 2001

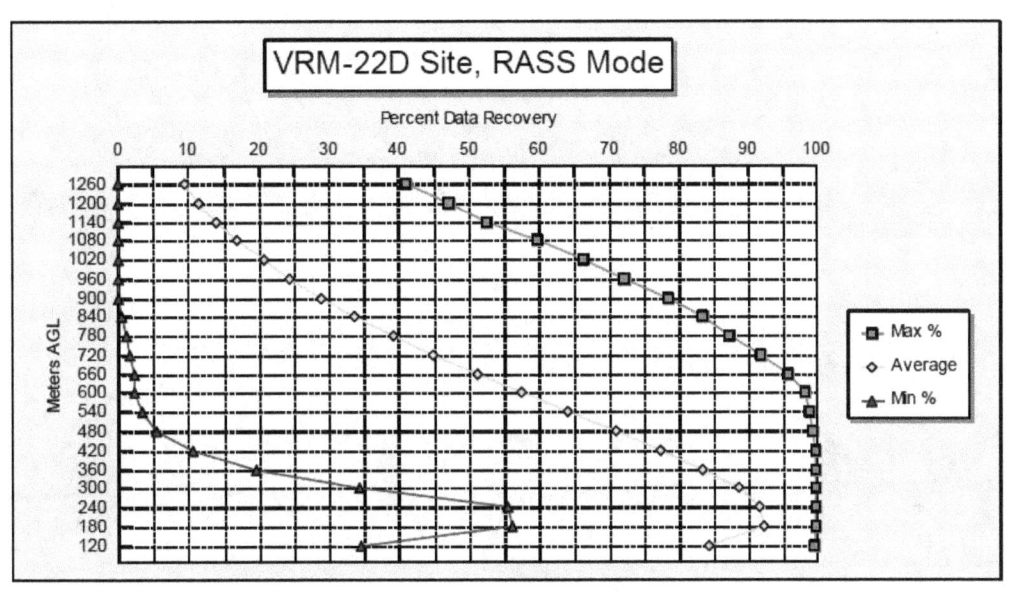

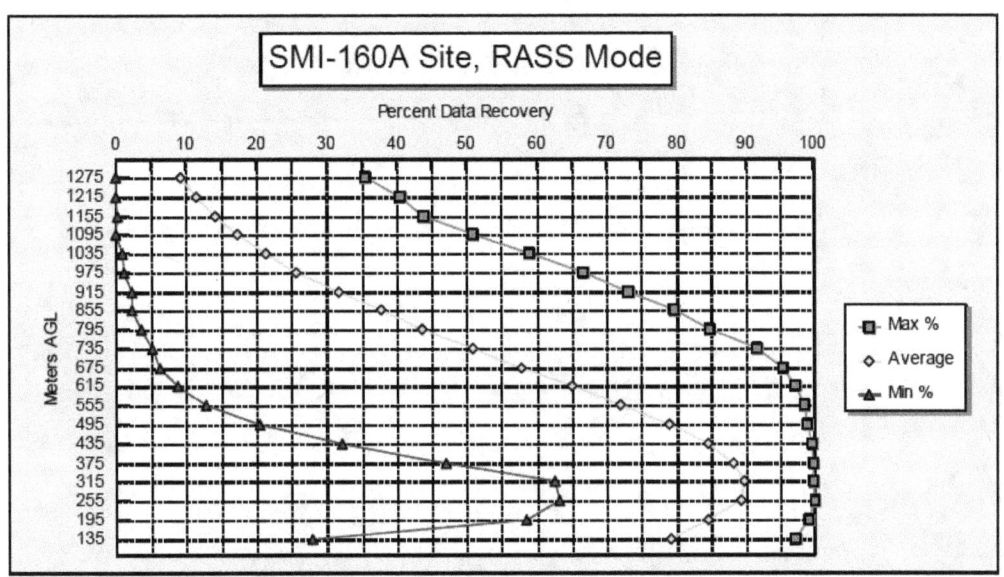

Figure 4-3. Data Recovery Rates for Radar Profiler RASS Mode, June 3, 1998 - October 2, 2001

5.0   EQUIPMENT PERFORMANCE AND DISPOSITION

All meteorological and communications equipment used in this data collection project were owned by MMS. The prime contractor was responsible for custody of all equipment during the preparation, installation, operation and maintenance, removal, and refurbishment phases of the project, as well as for return shipping of the equipment to MMS after the project.

5.1   Equipment Performance

The performance of all equipment used in the project was satisfactory, although failure experience varied as summarized below.

5.1.1   Upper Air Meteorological Measurement Equipment

The Radian (now Vaisala) radar profilers used to measure upper air winds and temperatures at the two project sites performed reliably throughout the 40-month data collection period, but experienced some hardware and software problems requiring project team corrective maintenance. Of note, neither of the two radar profilers were new at the beginning of the project and the component and configuration failure problems experienced during the project were within expected levels for equipment of this type, age, and interface with other sensor and communications devices.

Except for lightning damage repair to the VRM22D profiler in August 1999, the only hardware repairs required to the radar profilers during the project were the replacement of a power supply in the Radar Computer at SMI160A in January 2001 and the replacement of RF relays in the radar profiler's phase shifter in February 2001 at VRM22D and in May 2001 at SMI160A. Of note, the RF relays at both sites had more than fulfilled their life expectancy at the time of their respective failures at the two sites, and their required replacement was normal maintenance.

Software problems experienced were of several types and external causes. While none of the failures were due to deficiencies in the radar profiler software itself, the impacts experienced were manifest as radar profiler software interrupts. In one case, the interrupts were simultaneous at both sites, on 1/1/00 when the Global Positioning System (GPS) external device began telling the radar software that the year was 1900 rather than 2000 and both profilers stopped. This problem was difficult and time-consuming to identify, but was simple to fix and was a one-time problem. Throughout the data collection period, however, the radar profiler software experienced numerous interrupts caused by either the system's Radar Computer or Gateway Computer "hanging" while dealing with internal data transfer of radar profiler files and surface meteorological data files to the GOES Data Collection Platform (DCP). In each instance, the interrupts were quickly identified by the project team's data processing center and restoral action was initiated by the project team's field operations and maintenance personnel. These restorals were sometimes readily accomplished by system resets performed by remote dial-in to the computers via telephone modems. However, the required resets were frequently delayed while making multiple attempts to reach the modems or because platform personnel assistance was needed to perform the resets. Although platform personnel were always very cooperative and helpful, they were frequently not near a telephone to be reached or were reached but couldn't help until later because of higher priority duties in progress. As a problem class, the interrupts were largely a function of the then-current generation of Microsoft systems operating software in use not being capable of handling multi-tasking well. At the end of the project, the refurbishment of equipment provided for in the MMS contract included upgrades of the radar profiler software that now operate in a Windows NT environment, which is much more multi-tasking capable.

5.1.2   Surface Meteorological Equipment

A data logger and suite of wind, temperature, relative humidity (RH), pressure, and sea surface temperature (SST) sensors was used at each site to record surface meteorological data measurements throughout the 40-month data collection period. The data logger was connected to the site's Gateway Computer, part of the radar profiler equipment, for transmitting hourly observations into the site's GOES DCP.

The data logger at SMI160A operated without failure throughout the project. The data logger at VRM22D suffered confirmed lightning strike damage in August 1999 and suspected lightning strike damage in November 2000. Both instances resulted in outages that were corrected by replacing the damaged components. The VRM22D data logger also experienced one outage not related to lightning, which was a failed power supply that was replaced in March 2000.

The wind sensors initially provided by MMS were not robust enough to maintain reliable operation in platform site usage, and were replaced by a marine version at the beginning of the project. The only wind sensor problem experienced during the data collection period was that the VRM22D wind sensor failed to meet audit criteria in October 2000 and was replaced at that time.

The temperature/RH sensor at each site had to be replaced multiple times during the data collection period because of RH sensor data instability and/or failure to meet audit criteria. The RH sensor was the worst-performing of all sensors during the project. It had to be replaced six times at VRM22D and twice at SMI160A during project site visits, either because it had failed prior to the visit or because it failed to meet audit criteria during the visit.

The pressure sensor at each site performed without failure during the data collection period.

The SST sensor was the second-worst performing sensor during the data collection period. It had to be replaced three times at VRM22D and twice at SMI160A during the project during site visits, either because it had failed prior to the visit or because it failed to meet audit criteria during the visit. It also had to be replaced at VRM22D during one additional visit because the installed sensor was soon to need calibration.

5.1.3　　　　Supporting Communications and Other Equipment

Communications equipment used at each site included a telephone modem for as-needed remote connectivity to the Gateway Computer and a GOES Data Collection Platform (DCP) for hourly transmission of collected upper air and surface meteorological data. Supporting equipment used at each site included a GPS antenna/receiver for providing time stamp updates to the Radar and Gateway Computers and an Uninterruptible Power Supply (UPS) for providing backup power to the radar profiler to sustain operations during brief power outages.

The telephone modem at each site operated without failure during the project. However, multiple attempts were required to connect remotely to them because of the poor quality of the platform telephone lines.

Use of the GOES communications system, operated by NOAA's National Environmental Satellite Data and Information Services (NESDIS), made possible the near real-time retrieval of hourly measurements recorded at both project platform sites. Although the GOES communications system operated with a good up-time rate, there were periods during the 40-month data collection period when it was out of operation until restored by NESDIS. This occurred, for example, from March 30 to April 10, 2000.
A Synergetics GOES DCP unit was used at each site during the project to transmit data, collected by the Gateway Computer and relayed to the DCP, each hour to the GOES system. The DCP at VRM22D operated without failure throughout the project. The DCP at SMI160A, however, failed during installation and in October 1998, September 2000, and May 2001. In each case, it was replaced with the project's spare DCP and the failed unit was repaired and became the spare.

The GPS antenna/receiver used at each site to provide current time stamps to the Radar and Gateway Computers operated without hardware failure during the 40-month data collection period. However, on April 10, 1999 a platform power failure unfortunately occurred just as a GPS update was being made to the computers and they
"lost track of time" until the problem could be diagnosed and reset. More seriously, on January 1, 2000 the computers both stopped because the GPS began feeding them the year 1900 as part of time stamp updates. This Y2K problem in the GPS software was difficult to find, and data were lost from both sites until the cause was identified and a corrective visit to each platform site could be completed in mid-January 2000.

The UPS unit at each site provided battery-backup power that kept the radar profiler operating during platform power fluctuations and outages of less than about 20 minutes. No records are available to specify the number of such occurrences during which the UPS prevented downtime that would have otherwise occurred. However, platform power was observed to be less stable than typically experienced at similar land-based sites and the UPS units were therefore estimated to be very valuable to the project. Only one UPS hardware failure occurred during the project, when the unit at SMI160A experienced an internal battery malfunction in September 1999. It was removed during a site visit on September 30, 1999 and was re-installed during a site visit on 16 June 2000. No spare UPS unit was available for the project and repair time for the failed unit took longer than anticipated.

5.2 Equipment Disposition

During the data collection period, equipment refurbishment was performed on a continuous basis. Preventative maintenance routines were accomplished during every site visit to help assure optimal equipment performance. This included routine tasks such as checks and adjustments of outside equipment to maintain the physical alignment, orientation, and secure attachment of the radar profiler antennas and the surface meteorological sensors. It also included offload of computer data files to preclude their exceeding capacity limitations, and download of data from ZIP auxiliary data storage devices to provide backup data records. Equipment refurbishment was also conducted on an as-needed basis associated with corrective maintenance. This included spares replenishment by sending failed components and sensors to the respective manufacturers for repair in a timely manner after their removal from the platform sites during corrective maintenance visits. It also included having sensors recalibrated as needed in advance of calibration expiration dates.

After the completion of the data collection period, all equipment was removed from the platform sites and was shipped to the prime contractor's facility in Boulder, Colorado for inspection and applicable refurbishment prior to reshipment to MMS. Table 5-1 lists all MMS project equipment and shows refurbishment actions taken. For surface meteorological equipment, this included having sensors recalibrated as necessary to assure their readiness for any near term follow-on use by MMS in other field projects. For the radar profilers, this included selected component replacements and repair, as well as planned upgrade of the Radar Computers to current-technology LAP®-XM applications software and Windows NT® operating system software.

Table 5-1. Equipment Refurbishment

Equipment Type	Manufacturer/Model	Qty	Refurbishment Accomplished at Project Completion
Upper Air Meteorological Measurement Equipment			
Radar Profiler with RASS for upper air wind and temperature measurements	Vaisala LAP®3000 (including UPS unit and marine environmental upgrade)	2	LAP®-XM Software Upgrade (with Windows NT), wear and tear repair of outdoor components, and replacement of antenna relays and guy wires.
Spare Final Amplifier	Vaisala PN600010009	1	None required
Spare RASS Diaphram	Electro-Voice PN81157A	5	None required
Spare Fuses	Vaisala MDL-3, MDL-6, MDL-10	15	None required
Spare Radar Processor	Vaisala PN60011007	1	LAP®-XM Software
Spare Gateway Computer	Vaisala PN60001033	1	None required
Spare Phase Shifter	Vaisala PN40001024	1	None required
Spare Cable Set (excluding RASS)	Vaisala PN40001012, 40001013, 40004014, and 40004015	1	None required
Spare RASS Cable Set	Vaisala PN40001016	1	None required
Audio Amplifier	Peavey CS-800X	1	None required
Surface Meteorological Measurement Equipment			
Wind Direction and Speed Sensor	R.M. Young 05305 (non-marine model)	2	Calibration
Wind Direction and Speed Sensor	R.M. Young 05106-5 (marine model)	2	Calibration
Temperature/Relative Humidity Sensor	Campbell Scientific HMP35C	5	Calibration
Pressure Sensor	Vaisala	2	None required
Sea Surface Temperature (SST) Sensor	Everest Interscience 4000.4GL	4	Repair/Calibration (2) (The other two have valid calibration through 2003)
Cable for SST	Everest Interscience	3	None required
Serial Interface for SST	Vaisala PTA-427	3	None required

Table 5-1. Equipment Refurbishment (Cont'd)

Equipment Type	Manufacturer/Model	Qty	Refurbishment Accomplished at Project Completion
Data Logger	Campbell Scientific CR10	2	None required
Aspirator Radiation Shield	R.M Young 43408-2	2	None required
10-Meter Tower	Unknown UT930	2	None required
Mounting Hardware Set	Various	3	None required
Meteorological Sensor Calibration Kit	Unknown (1 barometer, 2 thermometer, 1 hygrometer)	1	Calibration
Communications and Data Storage Equipment			
GOES Data Collection Platform	Synergetics 3421A	3	None required
UDS Cellular Modem	Hayes Optima 14400	2	None required
UDS Cellular Modem	Accura 14400	1	None required
ZIP Data Storage Device	Iomega	2	None required

6.0   SUMMARY

The objective of this MMS project was to obtain field observations to better describe the vertical structure of the marine boundary layer over the Western and Central Gulf of Mexico for ongoing and future dispersion modeling applications. A three-year data collection period was originally planned, but was subsequently extended to 40 months by MMS. Data collection included hourly upper air and surface meteorological measurements recorded at two selected platform sites in the Gulf of Mexico, at respective distances of approximately 10km and 75km from the Louisiana shoreline.

A project team of contractor personnel performed all planning, data collection, and reporting work phases under the technical direction of the designated MMS COTR. A comprehensive Program Management Plan and a detailed Field Plan were prepared and approved at the beginning of the work effort and were kept current throughout the project. Progress reporting by the project team included monthly management reports throughout the contract period and monthly data reports throughout the 40-month data collection period.

With the concurrence of the respective platform owners, VRM22D was selected as the near-shore platform site and SMI160A was selected as the far-shore platform site. Support provided by the platform owners throughout the data collection period, at no cost to the project, included boat and helicopter transportation, space and power for the equipment, overnight accommodations for visiting project team personnel, and assistance by platform personnel with equipment installation, de-installation, and maintenance resets on a time-available basis.

Equipment used in the project is owned by MMS and included a 915 MHz pulsed-Doppler radar profiler, with RASS, at each site that provided upper air wind and virtual temperature measurements, a suite of surface meteorological sensors at each site that provided wind direction, wind speed, temperature, humidity, pressure, and sea surface temperature measurements, and a GOES Data Collection Platform at each site that provided the data transmission capability by which all measurements were retrieved each hour throughout the data collection period. At the end of the 40-month data collection period, the project team performed needed component refurbishment and sensor re-calibrations before returning the equipment to MMS.

All retrieved data measurements were received and quality controlled at the contractor's facility, and were also made available in near real-time to NOAA. As data receipt or quality problems were detected, project team personnel immediately attempted resolution by remote telephone modem contact with platform site equipment, and subsequently performed site corrective maintenance visits as required. In addition to these unscheduled site maintenance visits, scheduled audit visits to each site were also performed at approximately six month intervals throughout the 40-month data collection period.

The planned 40-month period of continuous data measurements was successfully completed on October 2, 2001. All equipment had been installed and tested by the project team at both sites by March 1998. However, the start of the data collection period was then delayed until June 3, 1998 while awaiting needed RF transmission site licenses for operating the radar profilers and for transmitting the data to the GOES satellite. With the exception of this unavoidable delay in the start date for the data collection period, all project work tasks were completed on schedule throughout the period of the contract.

The performance of the MMS-provided measurement equipment throughout the data collection period was satisfactory, although a number of operating interrupts and component failures were experienced. In each case these were resolved by project team personnel using remote telephone connection to the equipment when possible, or by performing a corrective maintenance site visit when necessary. During the 40-month data collection period, a total of 18 individual, unscheduled corrective maintenance site visits were required. In addition, project team personnel performed 14 scheduled audit visits, 7 to each site, during the 40-month period of operations. Equipment audits were also separately performed at each site following installation and prior to de-installation. Of all equipment used in the project, the relative humidity sensors and the sea surface temperature sensors were the least reliable. Relative humidity sensor replacements were required nine times and sea surface temperature replacements were required five times during the 40-month data collection period. External factors that most significantly limited equipment performance and maintenance during the project included platform power shutdowns for hurricane and tropical storm evacuations, lightning strikes and power fluctuations, active drilling on SMI160A during the last year of data collection, and the restricted availability of platform personnel or transportation to help support timely repairs.

The overall data capture rate achieved for the 40-month measurement period was 89.3%, which was slightly below the project goal of 90%. Since the 89.3% capture rate achieved did not vary significantly between upper air and surface meteorological data, or between sites, the predominant factor that impacted this rate was simply that platform sites were used, bringing into effect the types of challenges associated with remote site operations. Thanks in large measure to the outstanding help provided to the project team by platform personnel, within the limits permitted by their other duties, these remote site challenges were dealt with as effectively as possible during the data collection period and the overall data base assimilation objective of the project was successfully accomplished. Thanks to the efforts of all participants, the project was completed within budget and with no accidents.

7.0   REFERENCES

Ecklund, W.L., D.A. Carter, B.B. Balsley, P.E. Currier, J.L. Green, B.L. Weber, and K.S.Gage. 1990. Field tests of a lower tropospheric wind profiler. Radio Sci. 25: 899-906.

Fischler, M.A. and R.C. Bolles. 1981. Random sample consensus: A paradigm for model fitting with applications to image analysis and automated cartography. CACM 24/6. Pp. 381-395.

Lindsey, C.G., T.S. Dye, P.T. Roberts, J.A. Anderson, and S.E. Ray. 1995. Meteorological aspects of ozone episodes in southeast Texas. Paper No. 95-WP96.02 presented at the *Air & Waste Management Association 88th Annual Meeting, San Antonio, TX, June 18-23.*

U.S. Environmental Protection Agency. 1989. Quality assurance handbook for air pollution measurement systems, Volume IV - Meteorological Measurements. Prepared by Office of Research and Development, Atmospheric Research and Exposure Assessment Laboratory, Research Triangle Park, NC. EPA/600/4-90-003

Wuertz, D.B. and F.L. Weber. 1989. Editing wind profiler measurements. Prepared by NOAA/WPL, Boulder, CO. ERL 438-WPL 92.

The Department of the Interior Mission

As the Nation's principal conservation agency, the Department of the Interior has responsibility for most of our nationally owned public lands and natural resources. This includes fostering sound use of our land and water resources; protecting our fish, wildlife, and biological diversity; preserving the environmental and cultural values of our national parks and historical places; and providing for the enjoyment of life through outdoor recreation. The Department assesses our energy and mineral resources and works to ensure that their development is in the best interests of all our people by encouraging stewardship and citizen participation in their care. The Department also has a major responsibility for American Indian reservation communities and for people who live in island territories under U.S. administration.

The Minerals Management Service Mission

As a bureau of the Department of the Interior, the Minerals Management Service's (MMS) primary responsibilities are to manage the mineral resources located on the Nation's Outer Continental Shelf (OCS), collect revenue from the Federal OCS and onshore Federal and Indian lands, and distribute those revenues.

Moreover, in working to meet its responsibilities, the **Offshore Minerals Management Program** administers the OCS competitive leasing program and oversees the safe and environmentally sound exploration and production of our Nation's offshore natural gas, oil and other mineral resources. The MMS **Minerals Revenue Management** meets its responsibilities by ensuring the efficient, timely and accurate collection and disbursement of revenue from mineral leasing and production due to Indian tribes and allottees, States and the U.S. Treasury.

The MMS strives to fulfill its responsibilities through the general guiding principles of: (1) being responsive to the public's concerns and interests by maintaining a dialogue with all potentially affected parties and (2) carrying out its programs with an emphasis on working to enhance the quality of life for all Americans by lending MMS assistance and expertise to economic development and environmental protection.

www.ingramcontent.com/pod-product-compliance
Lightning Source LLC
Chambersburg PA
CBHW052000280526
45793CB00005B/795

* 9 7 8 1 5 0 5 5 0 5 7 7 1 *